The Zen Writings Series

ON ZEN PRACTICE II

ON ZEN PRACTICE II

BODY, BREATH AND MIND

**Edited by Hakuyu Taizan Maezumi
and Bernard Tetsugen Glassman**

Zen Writings Series

Zen Center Of Los Angeles

Publications of the Zen Center of Los Angeles

ZCLA Journal: Yasutani Roshi Memorial Issue
Zen and Science Issue

Zen Writings Series: On Zen Practice *(1976)*
On Zen Practice II *(1977)*
To Forget the Self: An Illustrated Introduction
To Zen Practice *(1977)*

The Zen Writings series is produced under the supervision of Series
Editors Taizan Maezumi Roshi and Tetsugen Glassman Sensei. *Publishing Editor:* John Daishin Buksbazen. *Design consultants:* Sy Edelstein,
Emmett Ho, John Daido Loori. *Contributing artists:* Tom Andrews,
Caribou, Sy Edelstein, Francis Haar, Emmett Ho, Manya Ekyo Maezumi,
Dan Morris, Frank Styduhar. *Production Staff:* Brenda Chiko Beck,
Stephan Ikko Bodian, Larry Jissan Christensen, Chris Ryogen Fang, Joan
Jōan George, Helen Glassman, Edward Kenzan Levin. *Distribution:* Paul
Genki Kahn. *Typesetting:* Valtype, Los Angeles, California. *Printing
and Binding:* Braun & Brumfield, Inc., Ann Arbor, Michigan.

This book was set in Press Roman type, and manufactured in the United
States of America.

On Zen Practice II is one volume in the Zen Writings series comprising two new titles
a year with occasional supplementary releases. Donation for two volumes a year: $7.00
in the U.S., $9.00 foreign. Single-volume donation: $4.00. For information about
subscriptions or distribution, contact Zen Writings, 927 South Normandie Avenue,
Los Angeles, California 90006. ISBN: 0-916820-04-1. Library of Congress Card Catalogue Number: 77-70251. Published by Zen Center of Los Angeles, Inc., 927 South
Normandie Avenue, Los Angeles, California 90006, a non-profit religious corporation.
© 1976 by Zen Center of Los Angeles, Inc. All rights reserved. Printed in the United
States of America.

CONTENTS

To The Reader:

Among the many books in English on Zen Buddhism, few are entirely based upon actual practice. Most deal with a variety of theoretical and cultural topics, while some set forth general principles of practice. This book and its previous companion volume, *On Zen Practice,* are a little different. They are a composite portrait of practice as conducted at the Zen Center of Los Angeles (ZCLA). Because Maezumi Roshi represents three distinct teaching traditions within Zen, there is a certain richness and diversity of approach. We have sought in these books to preserve something of the characteristic style and feel of ZCLA training. They reflect a living community, with personality and idiosyncracies left intact.

American Zen is taking root and growing strong; at times it is ungainly and raw, but it is also vigorous and unique in its own right. We offer these books to the reader, hoping to encourage others in their practice, and to afford the public a clearer, more accurate picture of what Zen practice is all about.

John Daishin Buksbazen
Publishing Editor

Ascending the high seat, (Dōgen Zenji) said: "There is in this assembly a man who has achieved a great enlightenment. Do you recognize him or not? If you do, come forward and ask me the Way. If you do not, you do not recognize him although you meet him face to face."

— Dōgen Zenji, *Eihei koroku*
(Translated by Taizan Maezumi Roshi)

Foreword
Chōtan Aitken Roshi

Once, many years ago, I heard a Buddhist priest speak at a
Bodhi Day ceremony to an assembly of congregations from all
Buddhist temples in Honolulu. His subject was the dual nature
of the Buddha-dharma: wisdom and compassion. To my great
disappointment, however, he could not bring these two themes
together. They remained separate, and a wonderful opportunity
to present the essence of deep realization was lost.

Truly, compassion and wisdom are the same thing. When
Bodhidharma came from India to China, Chih-kung, the advisor
to Emperor Wu of Liang, rightly identified him as the Mahasattva
Kuan-yin (Kannon). Since those early times, the archetypes of
Bodhidharma, with fierce discipline and consummate wisdom,
and Kannon, with androgynous visage and figure of love, have
reflected the two aspects of the same human being, wise
compassion and loving wisdom.

In these pages of *On Zen Practice II,* the timeless nature of
the Dharma as wisdom/compassion is vividly presented. Of
course, someone with a dangerous bit of learning may say the
same truth is expressed in raising a cup of tea or talking on the
telephone. True enough, but without the burning focus of the
polished glass we find here, and therefore with no power to save

anyone.

Wisdom/compassion is many things, but focus is the essential component of all of them. Ummon Bun'en Zenji (Yün-mên Wên-yen, d. 949 AD) taught by the model of a box and its lid. There must be a perfect fit. Reading the record of his instruction, we find a wide variety of styles. Each of his responses, however, like each of the responses of every authentic master, is cued to the time, the place, and the circumstances of the encounter. Included in the latter would be the exact nature of the student's need. You don't feed a baby a red pepper, no matter how hungry it may be. Such is the focus of wisdom/compassion. Such is the focus of these pages.

It is hard to meet an authentic master of Zen Buddhism, but here we have one in Taizan Maezumi Roshi. He is successor in the Dharma of all important streams of Zen, and has established an exemplary Zen center and gathered about him many talented disciples. There is no need to look further for a master of wisdom/compassion.

True mastery is many things. It is breadth of mind and spirit and the avoidance of division. Implicit in *On Zen Practice II* is acknowledgement that multiple themes, even disparate views, form the tapestry of correct Zen teaching. It is not shikan-taza alone, but also koan study. It is not the Soto or the Rinzai or the Harada stream, but all of them as a coherent and dynamic whole. It is not simply roshi, or even roshi and senior disciples, but roshi and all his students. It is not priest or lay person or scholar, but a community. Truly there are no barriers.

I have heard many teachers speak warmly of their own masters, quoting them continually. But in *On Zen Practice II*, we find a remarkable spectrum of Zen teachers, and we can sense the gratitude of Maezumi Roshi and his disciples to them all.

It is not a random selection, however. Beginning with Maezumi Roshi himself, these are talented and unique maestros of their art. Yasutani Roshi, one of Maezumi Roshi's principal masters, sacrificed all social prestige and devoted himself solely to teaching and writing, living in the lowliest of circumstances. His fiery convictions still burn fiercely in the spirit of his successors and on the pages of his many books.

Kōryū Ōsaka Roshi is an equally splendid master who was never ordained a priest. Like Yasutani Roshi, he has devoted himself to lay disciples, many of them college students. Maezumi Roshi studied with Kōryū Roshi also, first in his college days, and much later as a conclusion of his formal training. I haven't gotten to know Kōryū Roshi as well as I did Yasutani Roshi, but I remember him vividly from his one visit to the Maui Zendo, when a mild little man with the uncertainties of one almost blind suddenly became Mt. Fuji itself thundering the Dharma in a teisho.

Kōhun Yamada Roshi, brother of Maezumi Roshi in Yasutani Roshi's line, is my own Zen master. I know him to be an exacting teacher whose breadth of spirit matches Maezumi Roshi's own and attracts crowds of students of Christian as well as Buddhist origins to his modest dōjō in Kamakura.

Abe Masao Sensei is possessed of the same rare qualities we knew in Dr. D.T. Suzuki, a keen Zen eye and a scholarly mind. His writings on Dōgen Zenji are a primary resource for all Western students of Zen and Japanese thought. Prof. Norman Waddell is a colleague of Abe Sensei who collaborates with him on translations of Dōgen Zenji, and who translates other Zen works independently with clear insight into their fundamental meaning.

Finally, students at Zen Center are represented here with their expression of essential nature, inspired by Tetsugen Glassman Sensei in Dharma dialogue, and in the splendid production of this publication, in which John Daishin Buksbazen had a key role. We gain a vivid sense of enlightened Sangha spirit from them all.

We learn in Zen practice the infinitely precious nature of each particular entity, person, animal, plant, thing, and their complete equality. It is not an easy path. It is not easy to brush away the delusions that cloud emancipating truth. Without religious devotion, Zen becomes a kind of hobby. Without the great death and great rebirth, it becomes a kind of self-improvement exercise. It is not a subject to be mastered with a certain form or a certain curriculum, but a lifetime training. Yet with the devotion and rebirth so clearly manifest here, how easy it all is!

Introduction:
Can Everyone Realize His True Nature?

Taizan Maezumi Roshi

CAN everyone realize his true nature?

A: Before saying yes or no to this question, let us think about what one's "true nature" means. In our case, practicing together, we may say that it is a synonym of "Buddha-nature". As a matter of fact, this Buddha-nature or true nature of oneself is explained using such terms as: "original self", "original face", "Mind", sometimes "mu-ji", or "the cypress tree in the garden", or "thusness", or "reality", according to the context of the doctrine or the teachings.

When we consider this true nature as the Buddha-nature, it will clarify our understanding to observe the Buddha-nature from three different standpoints. The first one is called *shōin busshō,* the Buddha-nature inherent in all beings, whether enlightened or not. The next one is *ryōin busshō,* the Buddha-nature which is manifested when one begins to practice the Dharma. And the last is *enin busshō,* the Buddha-nature of one who has attained enlightenment.

Making an analogy, the *shōin busshō* is like gold which is in the ground. Regardless of whether or not people realize it, there is gold underground. The second one, *ryōin busshō,* is the Buddha-nature by virtue of which we are able to recognize where and how to extract the gold. The third one, *enin busshō,* is like whatever tools you use to take the gold out and get it into your hands. This is, of course, a very simple analogy of what Buddha-nature is, but it may tell you something.

Now, let's get back to your question, "Can everyone realize his true nature?"

In connection with the analogy, we may understand that all of us have the Buddha-nature, or rather, we are nothing *but* the Buddha-nature, and yet if we don't become aware that we already have the gold in our hands, we cannot be satisfied until we have it. So in order to have the gold in our hands, in order to realize our Buddha-nature, we have to do something, we have to make some effort. And if we really wish to do it, we will get it done sooner or later.

Q: But Roshi, in one of your teishos, you said some people will never get it. How do you explain this contradiction?

A: In order to answer this question, let me return to the analogy I made. Everybody knows that gold is someplace in the ground; in some places there is this gold, and in other places there is not, and if we dig in the wrong place to get the gold, it is in vain, regardless of how hard we try. So in order to realize this Buddha-nature, we have to have the right means and the right direction in which to pursue our efforts to find the gold.

Q: What would be the right direction?

A: Let's reflect upon the words of Dōgen Zenji: "It is not a matter of being smart or dull, well-learned or foolish, but if one practices whole-heartedly to find out what the Way is, that is nothing but the accomplishment of the Way." The point is this: straight-forward whole-heartedness in accord with one's practice. These famous words of Dōgen Zenji, *isshiki no bendō,* mean "To practice the Way with whole-heartedness", or "to become one with whatever you do." In other words, *to become one is the key. When you really become one with whatever you do, that is the realization of the Way.* So that whether everyone realizes his true nature or not is dependent on the individual.

Even being lazy and not doing anything still is nothing but the Buddha-nature. That is to say, one has gold and yet he does not think so, so he simply does not realize his own nature. There is a famous analogy by the Buddha: A very poor man had a friend who was very rich. One time they met together, enjoyed a few drinks, and eventually the poor man fell asleep. Looking at this poor man, the rich friend felt sorry for him, and without letting him know, slipped a precious jewel into his garment. After parting from his rich friend, this poor man returned again to his life as a beggar without knowing he had that precious jewel. After some time they met again and the rich friend was surprised and asked him: "I gave you that jewel; why did you not use it to make your life comfortable?" And the poor man said, "No, you never gave me anything!" So the rich friend reached into the garment where he put the jewel, took it out, and showed it to him. This analogy may tell you something.

Q: How can we strengthen our faith in order to practice better?

A: Once again this is a very fundamental thing. Faith is a very fundamental, very important matter in life, so this question permits me to say that to strengthen our faith is practically always a synonym for bettering our practice.

When we have faith, it is necessary to examine in what we put our faith. We have a proverb, "To believe in the head of a dried, dead sardine has power to chase away evil spirits." As a matter of fact, we believe in all sorts of different things, and we put our faith in different things, such as money, fame, ideas, thoughts, ideologies, emotions, feelings. So, in order to practice better, we must have our faith in the right way. And what is the right way? To put our faith in whatever the Buddha and the Patriarchs say. To put ourselves whole-heartedly into it and practice diligently. So, in connection with the previous question, have strong faith in yourself, in the fact that your life is itself nothing but Buddha-nature. To have strong faith in this fact and to practice in accordance with what the Buddha and the Patriarchs say, leads us to better practice and strengthens our faith. It is also important to renew our vows from time to time and to encourage ourselves to accomplish further. By doing so we can strengthen our faith, and this faith, again, better promotes our practice. It is like a circle. There is this famous doctrine: first, *hosshin,* to raise the bodhi-mind or seek for realization; second, *shugyō,* practice; third, *bodai,* attainment of realization; fourth, *nehan,* nirvana. In the state of nirvana lies the bodhi-mind, then again practice, then attainment, then nirvana, spiraling ever upward. Dōgen Zenji said that our practice is like a spiral comprising these four strands.

Shugyō (practice)

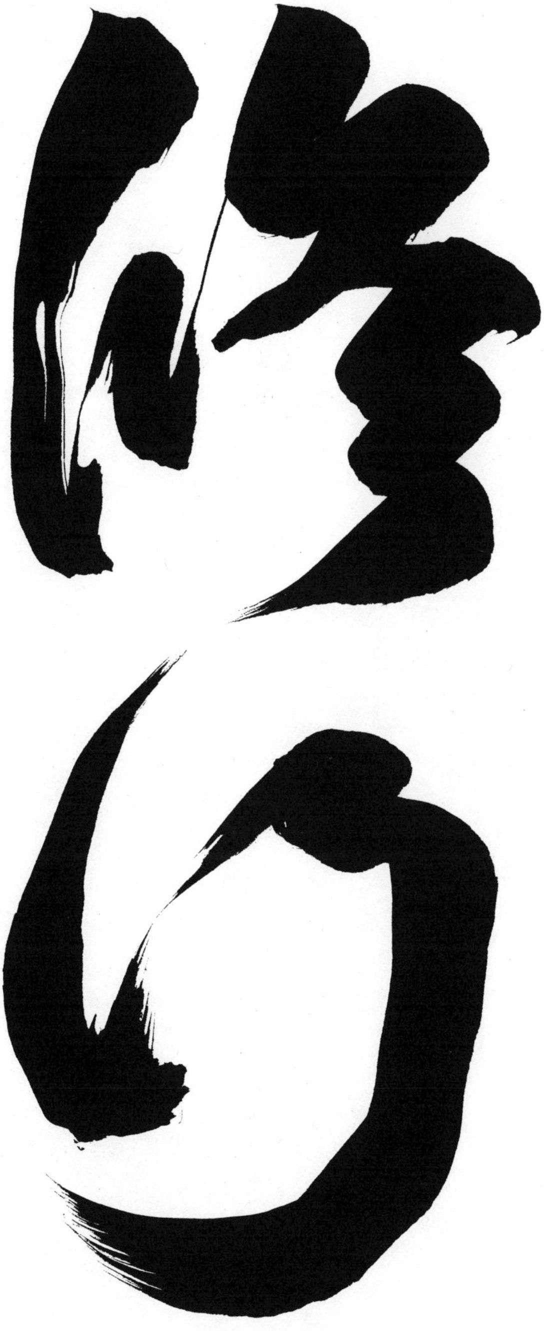

CHAPTER 1
Dōgen Zenji and Enlightenment
Kōhun Yamada Roshi

FIRST of all I must give my deep gratitude to Maezumi Roshi for giving me this opportunity to come here to see all of you. This evening I am going to speak in Japanese and Maezumi Roshi will translate for you.

Among Japanese Buddhists there are quite a few who believe that Dōgen Zenji's Zen is a very special Zen which does not particularly require an enlightenment or satori experience. Even among priests and monks quite a few believe so.

To state my conclusion first, such a belief is a mistake. I firmly believe that the most important matter of Buddhism is to get enlightenment. The point by which Zen Buddhism is differentiated from other religions or philosophies and from all kinds of theories, is this: the attainment of enlightenment. The most important thing in our practice is this enlightenment, and this is not found in other systems. When you carefully examine Dōgen Zenji's writings, it is simply impossible to understand how people can say that sort of thing. For example, if we read an article, a very famous chapter of the *Shōbōgenzō* called "Bendōwa", or the *Fukanzazengi,* (Instructions on Zazen to All), we repeatedly find that Dōgen Zenji emphasizes the importance of attaining enlightenment and having the kensho experience.

In some parts of his writings, however, he also mentions that without paying much attention to attaining enlightenment, we should just try to sit. We call that aspect shikan-taza. And how we connect with shikan-taza, to just sit, that is what I want to explain. To speak as simply as possible, I rather wish to use this parable or analogy in order to clarify this point.

Dōgen Zenji always stands at the highest peak and tries to lead the students up to his level, so I will try to explain this using the analogy of school education. I understand that in this country you don't have very much trouble with entrance examinations for public schools; but in Japan, along with your progress in elementary school, in order to go on to middle school you must take an examination. Next, in order to go to high school you have another examination, and to enter college, yet another one which is very difficult. Thus young people in Japan study hard to get into the better schools. Dōgen Zenji, first of all, speaks to those who are the very best among all students. He expects them to be the finest of scholars, so that regardless of how difficult the entrance examination for high school or for college, it is a prerequisite for them to go through such barriers.

I mentioned the examination, which, as you might guess, refers to the kensho experience. Dōgen Zenji's position is that he expects those who are involved in practice to achieve the highest peak—where he stands. Accordingly, in the process of such achievement, having a kensho experience is so basic a prerequisite that consequently he does not put much emphasis on it. Continuing the analogy, the Rinzai School, of course, aims at an accomplishment such as becoming a fine scholar. However, if your ability won't even get you through the high school entrance examination, then the more advanced accomplishment is out of the question. First, you must enroll in high school, passing the entrance examination, which is kensho. That is the reason the Rinzai School emphasizes the importance of having a kensho experience. And yet, among those who practice Rinzai Zen we see quite a few who quit after having their first kensho experience.

Of course, this is not right practice either, and both Soto and Rinzai Schools aim at the highest levels of achievement. However, as I mentioned before, Dōgen Zenji, expecting all of us to achieve that highest level, does not put too much emphasis on such preliminary stages of achievement. Accordingly, he appears to be giving less emphasis to the importance of the kensho experience than does the Rinzai School. Therefore, I should like to emphasize again the importance of having kensho experience. Without this, there is practically no Zen Buddhism.

Let me make another analogy: suppose there is a three-story building. The first floor is the domain in which we usually live; the second floor is somewhat similar to the position of the Rinzai School, which is the state of attaining enlightenment; and the third floor is the domain to which Dōgen Zenji summons us. Of course, in order to come up to the third floor, you have to go by way of the second floor. So, for Dōgen Zenji it is very natural to expect the students to go through the second floor to come up to the third. And, since in the Rinzai School they emphasize having the kensho experience (which is reaching the second floor), some people quit after getting up to the second floor, which is not quite right practice either.

However, those Rinzai roshis with really clear vision know very well that all of us have to go to the third floor. And again, as a matter of fact, above the third floor there are boundless skies expanding. That simply implies that our practice is to accomplish and to clarify ourselves endlessly. Many people say Dōgen Zenji is very difficult to understand. In connection with the difficulty of his writings I should like to explain what enlightenment is.

All of us are living right now in this room. Suppose we imagine that this room is the space in which we usually live; then we might say that the walls are the walls of common sense. Please imagine all the walls, ceiling, floor, covered by very dark glass. Since it is so dark and completely black, one does not know there is a world outside of this. However, by reading books written by Buddhist scholars and Zen masters, and attending meetings such as this, one starts to think that seemingly another world exists besides the limited space in this room. The writings of masters are the records of the external world and also its relation to the inside of this room. Finally, one comes to the point that there *must* be some different world existing outside this room. And to *see* the world which is outside this limited room, that means to achieve, or to have the experience of kensho.

In order to see the outside world, we most commonly use koans such as mu-ji. To work on mu-ji is something like making a little hole in that glass. As a result of trying to make a hole through that dark glass, you will succeed and will make a little hole. Sometimes, even a great big part of the glass may shatter. Such is to be called the Great Enlightenment.

By making a small hole through which you can see the outside world, even though the hole is very small, such experience could be called kensho. Even having a small kensho experience, and then to continue making very tiny holes in the glass, going through the koan practice afterward, you can make that hole gradually bigger and bigger. And again, continuing that effort, eventually you can eliminate all the glass. Such a stage is called Perfect Enlightenment. When you achieve this state, you will see clearly that from the beginning, there was no such thing as that which you believed yourself to be surrounded by: no glass walls, ceiling, floor. There was no such limitation from the beginning, that was mere illusion and delusion. The masters, such as Dōgen Zenji, really realized this fact: that from the beginning there is no such bondage or restriction. Even, though, for those who have had so-called kensho, since such experience is still very limited, you cannot quite realize what the next room is all about. In other words, still there is a division between this room and the next room, or this space and the next world, the space outside. This inside world is the so-called phenomenal world, and the outside world, the so-called substantial, original world.

Even though fairly well accomplished in one's practice, it is rather common to say that there is some kind of division between this room and the other room, or next room. It just feels like there is a very thin screen preventing you from really realizing thoroughly that there is no division. However, a great master like Dōgen Zenji says there is not even a very thin division which separates him from the outside world.

Being completely free, Dōgen Zenji talks about this room in one sentence, and about the outside world in the next. Since there is no division, he is so free to talk about either of them, that when people read it *without* such freedom, they have to guess and try hard to understand. And the average reader thinks that Dōgen Zenji is talking about this room, and then in the very next line he is talking about the other side, and then again this side, freely switching back and forth. So Dōgen Zenji's freedom causes difficulties for people to really follow his thought because of their own limitations.

There are other difficulties in Dōgen Zenji's writings. Because of the originality of his thought, he often invents words to express his meaning, or alters conventional Buddhist terminology. But it is his freedom that I want you to be especially aware of at this point.

I should like to mention one more analogy, involving the ocean. I want you to imagine some kind of aquatic animal which also has wings and can fly up into the air. Since that particular animal was born, he has been just dwelling in the water and does not know the other worlds. Somehow, while he is growing up, he is told by his seniors that there is another world besides water, which is called the sky. This animal wants to see the sky and what kind of thing it could be. And, from the very deep ocean bottom, he tries to come up to the surface of the water. That effort is like the practice of your zazen. Approaching the surface of the water, eventually he pokes his head out. The instance of such an experience is to be called kensho.

Now you can imagine what a delightful experience it would be for the one who hadn't previously known such a world at all, having only lived in the water. Somehow he experiences a completely different world. After that, he still continues to improve himself, becoming very free, flying in the sky and diving in the ocean, dwelling in the air, and also living in the water. After having such kensho experience, you just keep on your practice, then become quite free to be in either sphere. Such a state is called Perfect Enlightenment. And after attaining complete enlightenment, making yourself completely free, you realize that, from the beginning, there was no division between the air and the water, the sky and the ocean, even though from the surface it seemed divided.

Being completely free, Dōgen Zenji describes these matters by one moment talking about the water and the next moment about the sky. For him, practically, there is no division. The way he sees is quite different from how ordinary people see, which makes his writings very difficult for the reader to follow and comprehend.

But, returning to my earlier analogy, once we have passed through the second floor and have reached the third, then we live side by side with Dōgen Zenji. Then we can see freely in all directions, and his wisdom is no longer inaccessible to us, but is our own.

Thank you for listening.

CHAPTER 2

Fukanzazengi   (The Universal Promotion of the Principles of Zazen) by Dōgen Zenji

Translated by Norman Waddell and Abe Masao

THE WAY is basically perfect and all-pervading. How could it be contingent upon practice and realization? The Dharma-vehicle is free and untrammeled. What need is there for man's concentrated effort? Indeed, the Whole Body is far beyond the world's dust. Who could believe in a means to brush it clean? It is never apart from one right where one is. What is the use of going off here and there to practice?

And yet, if there is the slightest discrepancy, the Way is as distant as heaven from earth. If the least like or dislike arises, the Mind is lost in confusion. Suppose one gains pride of understanding and inflates one's own enlightenment, glimpsing the wisdom that runs through all things, attaining the Way and clarifying the Mind, raising an aspiration to escalade the very sky. One is making the initial, partial excursions about the frontiers but is still somewhat deficient in the vital Way of total emancipation.

Need I mention the Buddha, who was possessed of inborn knowledge? —the influence of his six years of upright sitting is noticeable still. Or Bodhidharma's transmission of the mind-seal?

Translation reprinted from *Eastern Buddhist*, Vol. VI, No. 2, October, 1973.

—the fame of his nine years of wall-sitting is celebrated to this day. Since this was the case with the saints of old, how can men of today dispense with negotiation of the Way?

You should therefore cease from practice based on intellectual understanding, pursuing words and following after speech, and learn the backward step that turns your light inwardly to illuminate your self. Body and mind of themselves will drop away, and your original face will be manifest. If you want to attain suchness, you should practice suchness without delay.

For *sanzen* a quiet room is suitable. Eat and drink moderately. Cast aside all involvements and cease all affairs. Do not think good or bad. Do not administer pros and cons. Cease all the movements of the conscious mind, the gauging of all thoughts and views. Have no designs on becoming a buddha. [Sanzen] has nothing whatever to do with sitting or lying down.

At the site of your regular sitting, spread out thick matting and place a cushion above it. Sit either in the full-lotus or half-lotus position. In the full-lotus position, you first place your right foot on your left thigh and your left foot on your right thigh. In the half-lotus, you simply press your left foot against your right thigh. You should have your robes and belt loosely bound and arranged in order. Then place your right hand on your left leg and your left palm [facing upwards] on your right palm, thumb-tips touching. Thus sit upright in correct bodily posture, neither inclining to the left nor to the right, neither leaning forward nor backward. Be sure your ears are on a plane with your shoulders and your nose in line with your navel. Place your tongue against the front roof of your mouth, with teeth and lips both shut. Your eyes should always remain open, and you should breathe gently through your nose.

Once you have adjusted your posture, take a deep breath, inhale and exhale, rock your body right and left and settle into a steady, immobile sitting position. Think of not-thinking. How do you think of not-thinking? Non-thinking. This in itself is the essential art of zazen.

The zazen I speak of is not learning meditation. It is simply the Dharma-gate of repose and bliss, the practice-realization of totally culminated enlightenment. It is the manifestation of ul-

timate reality. Traps and snares can never reach it. Once its heart
is grasped, you are like the dragon when he gains the water, like
the tiger when he enters the mountain. For you must know that
just there [in zazen] the right Dharma is manifesting itself and
that from the first dullness and distraction are struck aside.

When you arise from sitting, move slowly and quietly, calmly
and deliberately. Do not rise suddenly or abruptly. In surveying
the past, we find that transcendence of both unenlightenment
and enlightment, and dying while either sitting or standing, have
all depended entirely on the strength [of zazen].

In addition, the bringing about of enlightenment by the opportunity provided by a finger, a banner, a needle, or a mallet,
and the effecting of realization with the aid of a *hossu*, a fist, a
staff, or a shout, cannot be fully understood by man's discriminative thinking. Indeed, it cannot be fully known by the practicing or realizing of supernatural powers either. It must be de-
portment beyond man's hearing and seeing — is it not a principle
that is prior to his knowledge and perceptions?

This being the case, intelligence or lack of it does not matter;
between the dull and the sharp-witted there is no distinction. If
you concentrate your effort singlemindedly, that in itself is negotiating the Way. Practice-realization is naturally undefiled.
Going forward [in practice] is a matter of everydayness.

In general, this world and other worlds as well, both in India
and China, equally hold the Buddha-seal, and over all prevails
the character of this school, which is simply devotion to sitting,
total engagement in immobile sitting. Although it is said that
there are as many minds as there are men, still they (all) negotiate the Way solely in zazen. Why leave behind the seat that
exists in your home and go aimlessly off to the dusty realms of
other lands? If you make one misstep you go astray from (the
Way) directly before you.

You have gained the pivotal opportunity of human form. Do
not use your time in vain. You are maintaining the essential
working of the Buddha Way. Who would take wasteful delight
in the spark from the flintstone? Besides, form and substance
are like the dew on the grass, destiny like the dart of lightning —
emptied in an instant, vanished in a flash.

Please, honored followers of Zen. Long accustomed to groping for the elephant, do not be suspicious of the true dragon.
Devote your energies to a way that directly indicates the absolute. Revere the man of complete attainment who is beyond all
human agency. Gain accord with the enlightenment of the buddhas; succeed to the legitimate lineage of the patriarchs' samadhi.
Constantly perform in such a manner and you are assured of
being a person such as they. Your treasure-store will open of
itself, and you will use it at will.

CHAPTER 3
Commentary on Dōgen Zenji's *Fukanzazengi*
Taizan Maezumi Roshi

DŌGEN ZENJI wrote the *Fukanzazengi* between October and December of the year 1227, at the age of 28, just after he had returned from China. He had done koan study under Master Eisai for a year until Master Eisai passed away, then studied under Eisai Zenji's first successor, Priest Myōzen, for about nine years. Following this, he went to China with Priest Myōzen and stayed there for about four years.

Now this is a very important point: even though Dōgen Zenji doesn't emphasize koan study very much, actually he studied koans himself for nine years. Then, going further, he attained a more thorough enlightenment under Tendō Nyojō in China, after which he stayed with Master Tendō a couple of years more. When Master Dōgen returned to Japan, this work, the *Fukanzazengi,* may well have been his very first work. It was after this he wrote the *Shōbōgenzō.*

But Dōgen Zenji actually had two *Shōbōgenzō*s: the one to which we usually refer, which he wrote in Japanese, and another, which he wrote in Chinese. The Chinese version was actually a compilation of some three hundred classical koans, which he

may have studied under Priest Myōzen, as well as under Master
Eisai. But somehow or other, until as recently as perhaps only
twenty or thirty years ago, the present-day Soto School has
managed to overlook these three hundred koans.

Nonetheless, Dōgen Zenji used koans quite commonly, not to
mention his use of numerous passages from the sutras which he
quoted in koan-like manner. Strictly speaking, you cannot really
appreciate the *Shōbōgenzō* without an understanding of koans.

Of course, you can interpret koans according to your knowledge, but such mere interpretation is not so good. You should
have your own realization.

The title of this work, *Fukanzazengi,* could be translated in a
number of ways. Dr. Abe has translated it as "The Universal
Promotion of the Principles of Zazen." The thing to understand
about the title is that, first of all, Dōgen Zenji isn't just giving a
lecture on how to do zazen; he is really urging everybody to do
it. And he uses the word *fukan* in the title to convey the univer-
sality of these principles, applying them without exception to all
beings. Of course, we emphasize sitting; we say "just sit". But
merely putting your body in a sitting position isn't quite enough.
Sitting is *zazen,* or *za + zen,* "sitting Zen". At least, it's supposed
to be so. And that raises the question of what is Zen? But anyway, our practice should be real zazen.

And yet, zazen can be done by anybody, everybody. In order
to do zazen, we don't need to have anything more than a body.
That much is quite sufficient.

When Dōgen Zenji returned to Japan from his stay in China,
even though Zen had already come to Japan, he wasn't quite
satisfied with the kind of Zen practice then being done. He
sensed that the Zen of Japan at that time was somehow less
accurate, less vital than it should be. For example, Eisai Zenji
himself combined the principles of Zen and the teachings of the
Tendai and Shingon Schools. So it wasn't really genuine classical
zazen being taught and practiced.

But Dōgen Zenji, after his great realization under Master
Tendō, .was very strongly convinced that just straight zazen
should be very genuinely practiced. When you study his work,
you'll see what strong language he used to convey this. At any

rate, in writing this, Dōgen Zenji wanted not only to promote the practice of zazen as such, but to encourage people to do the kind of genuine zazen which Master Dōgen had himself experienced and come to understand.

It is characteristic of Dōgen Zenji's writing style that he says the most important thing immediately, in the first couple of lines or in the first paragraph. That is where he states his central idea or theme.

Yasutani Roshi once told me that Harada Roshi used to stress the significance of the opening words of the *Fukanzàzengi.* They are *"Tazunuru ni sore. . .",* and can be translated roughly as "After searching exhaustively. . ." In almost all English translations available today, this introductory phrase is not translated at all, being regarded as an untranslatable formal opening. But that may not be quite correct in this instance, for it greatly affects the meaning of the first paragraph. The sense of the opening passage is something like "After searching exhaustively, (or 'After a thorough search for the truth') he came to the realization that the very essence of the Way is originally perfect and all-pervading." Dr. Abe uses the word "basically" as an adverb. But the same character, *moto,* could also be translated as a noun: the "origin of the Way." Or we could read it as the "fundamental Way." And why is it said to be the fundamental Way? It is because it is universal; it is all-pervading; it is complete. Then what is it? Sunyata, emptiness, or Buddha-nature. That is our life.

All of us are here to find our true self or the real implication of life and death. But here it says, "After searching exhaustively, the very essence or origin of the Way is perfect and all-pervading." What is the Way? In technical terms, it's *anuttara samyak sambodhi,* the Supreme Enlightenment. In Chinese it's translated as the "Supreme Way", the "very best Way", the "unsurpassable Way," or as "Perfect Wisdom," which is what enlightenment actually is. So enlightenment is synonymous with the Way. The Supreme Way (or complete realization) is perfect in itself, by itself.

And again, we may àsk, "What is wisdom? What is *anuttara samyak sambodhi?*" It is our life itself. We not only have that wisdom; we are constantly using it. When it's cold, we put on more clothing. When it's hot, we take our clothes off. When hungry, we eat. When sad, we cry. Being happy, we laugh. That's wisdom. And it doesn't only pertain to humans, either, but to anything and everything. Birds chirp, dogs run, mountains are high, valleys low. It's all wisdom! The seasons change, the stars shine in the heavens; it's wisdom. Regardless of whether we realize it or not, we are always in the midst of the Way. Or, more strictly speaking, we are nothing but the Way itself.

Of course, there are always reasons and causes for our being the way we are. The Law of Causation applies to everybody; no one really escapes from it. In a sense, it's everything. So the key is actually how clearly we realize the Way, which is, after all, nothing but ourselves. And realizing that the Way is all-pervading, perfect and complete, what have we to worry about? In the Soto School, our emphasis is more on this original realization or fundamental enlightenment which is nothing but our life itself. Then what we should do is take care of it and not stain or defile it. Whatever we do then becomes the act of the Buddha.

That's what the first line refers to when it says". . . the Way is complete and all-pervading. How could it be contingent on practice and realization?"

THE DHARMA-VEHICLE is free and untrammeled.
What need is there for man's concentrated effort?

Actually here he is saying the same thing again. The vehicle on which we carry this very essence of life is totally free, without bondage or restriction. That vehicle is nothing but our life. So our life is also originally free, unrestricted. Of course, as long as we are alive we have to live under certain conditions, which, in a sense, is a limitation. But within limitation there is always freedom. Regardless of where you go or what you do, in one way or another your life is restricted. So if you look to circumstances or to environment for your freedom, that's the wrong attitude. You always find freedom within limitation.

THE DHARMA-VEHICLE is free and untrammeled.
What need is there for man's concentrated effort? Indeed, the Whole Body is far beyond the world's dust.

Who could believe in a means to brush it clean?

In this passage, the word "world's" is unnecessary. Just "far beyond dust." We have all sorts of dust, but altogether it's far beyond dust. This is a nice koan.

"The Whole Body." What is the Whole Body? Again, it's nothing but the body of each of us. Each one of us must go beyond all sorts of dust. It's unnecessary to wipe off the dust as such. Isn't it nice?

That reminds me of the famous passage from the *Platform Sutra,* where it quotes the verses of both the Sixth Patriarch and Priest Jinshu (Shen Hsiu).

Priest Jinshu's verse went:

> Our body is the Bodhi tree,
> And our mind a mirror bright.
> Carefully we wipe them hour by hour,
> And let no dust alight.

And the Sixth Patriarch responded to that poem:

> There is no Bodhi tree,
> Nor the stand of a mirror bright.
> Since all is void,
> Where can the dust alight?

You see? It's not a matter of dusting off, or of shining or polishing. Our original self, original nature, or whatever we call it, *that is the Way.* Dōgen Zenji says the same thing. The Way, the body, is complete, perfect, free, all-pervading.

> It is never apart from one right where one is. What is
> the use of going off here and there to practice?

It's very important. Always here. From time to time I mention, always right here and right now. And it's the same for all of you. Always, wherever you go, wherever you are, it's right here, and right now, complete, free, all-pervading. Isn't it wonderful? That is our life. So just be so; be so. Don't defile it or stain it.

AND YET, if there is the slightest discrepancy, the Way is as distant as heaven from earth. If the least like or dislike arises, the Mind is lost in confusion. Suppose one gains pride of understanding and inflates one's own enlightenment, glimpsing the wisdom that runs through all things, attaining the Way and clarifying the Mind, raising an aspiration to escalade the very sky. One is making the initial, partial excursions about the frontier, but is still somewhat deficient in the vital Way of total emancipation.

The first sentence of this paragraph has a double meaning; you can take it literally and also look at its hidden implication. But if you understand that the Way is fundamentally perfect, complete, free, all-pervading, then you understand what it means.

In a way, "all-pervading" is a correct translation of the word *zu,* but perhaps "free" might be better. One definition of *zu,* or "penetration", is "unhindered functioning." When we say "all-pervading," we think of something like gravity, which exists all over, everywhere. Taken in that sense, it becomes rather passive, static. But its functioning is really an active, positive thing.

Before we go further, let me explain the two aspects of our practice and our life: the intrinsic, or underlying; and the practical, or experiential. On the level of the intrinsic, we are dealing with an ultimate reality; the way things really are, whether or not we are aware of it.

On the practical or experiential level, we are dealing with what we have directly and consciously experienced and know directly to be the case.

So looking at this passage from the experiential perspective, it is obvious that if we don't practice correctly, if we don't experience it rightly, then we miss the point. And so we create the difference, the distance between ourselves and externals, and cannot recognize the Way.

But when we examine it from the intrinsic perspective, just being as we are is perfect. Perhaps the word "perfect" is not quite adequate; let me use the word "complete". Nothing is lacking; nothing is in excess. No two things can be identical. Each one of us is distinctly different. That's what it means. When there is the slightest difference, then it becomes as separate as heaven from earth. That means our individual existence or being is absolute and obvious, as clear as the separation between heaven and earth. So the hidden implication of this line is that each of us is perfect and free from that very fundamental perspective; it is a very strong affirmation of our life. And the point of our practice is not to become something other than what we already are, such as a Buddha or enlightened person, but to realize or become aware of the fact that we *are* intrinsically, originally the Way itself, which is free and complete. If we practice to become something else, we simply put another head on top of our own, thus becoming a ghost. One head is enough.

So then, how do we realize that our life is complete and free? Or, how clearly do we realize that point? That's the point of our practice.

Dōgen Zenji says, "To study the Enlightened Way is to study the self. And to study the self is to forget the self." To forget the self is not to create any distance between oneself and the Way. Then what makes for such distance?

What creates the distance is always that limited ego-consciousness. With consciousness *per se* there is nothing at all wrong. It's a very plain, pure functioning of the body, and not a matter of right or wrong. We've got to have it. But our trouble is that we give too much value, too much authority to one particular part of our conscious functioning. We think that we can figure out everything by our intelligence, by our thinking, by our ideas and thoughts and concepts. Then we get into trouble.

So eliminate or set aside those ideas and preconceived notions. Just stop that entire process of analysis and idea formation, that's what Dōgen Zenji says.

> If the least like or dislike arises, the Mind is lost in confusion.

In other words, when you start having ideas of liking or disliking, right or wrong, good or bad, enlightened or deluded, then you lose the Mind. Again, this Mind can be seen as synonymous with the Way. You become apart from the Way.

SUPPOSE ONE GAINS pride of understanding and inflates one's own enlightenment, glimpsing the wisdom that runs through all things, attaining the Way and clarifying the Mind, raising an aspiration to escalade the very sky. One is making the initial, partial excursions about the frontiers, but it is still somewhat deficient in the vital Way of total emancipation.

If you look at the Ten Oxherding Pictures, it may help you to understand the rest of this paragraph. The point is this: even attaining very clear enlightenment, still such attainment or such a state is just a beginning. We say, "the head is through, but the' body is still sticking out." In other words, still a very early, premature state. Attaining enlightenment, clear vision, wisdom, seeing that the whole world is nothing but myself, such understanding is nothing but the beginning. And while you are stuck in that kind of place, then you have fallen into the ocean of poison and can never liberate yourself. In the Ten Oxherding Pictures, this stage corresponds to the third one, seeing the ox. And after seeing the ox, we still have much to do. Catching the ox, the fourth stage, is the Great Enlightenment. And if we loosely interpret what Dōgen Zenji is talking about here in the second paragraph, we could say it is at the level of the fourth stage. But if we strictly interpret it, even such clear enlightenment as this is still the third stage. And koan practice as such is the second stage.

I remember one time Yasutani Roshi was telling us, those who have finished koan study and have been approved by their teacher, maybe are barely at the third stage. So we can interpret it in different ways.

That's what Dōgen Zenji says; even though having clear enlightenment and feeling terrific, yet at such a stage, it's just like poking your nose into something. You aren't at all free.

We might remember the story of Hakuin Zenji, who at the age of 24 years, attained very clear enlightenment upon hearing the temple gong ring at dawn. He was just as Dōgen Zenji has described here: caught by the terrific sensation of delight and the thought that nobody in the last hundred years had had such a clear enlightenment as he. Much later, reflecting upon his youth, he wrote of this experience that conceit and arrogance came up just like the ocean tide. Later on, he came across Shōju Roshi, who deflated him thoroughly and helped him attain a clearer second realization.

But anyway, regarding this paragraph, what Dōgen Zenji is saying is that we must be careful about how we proceed in our practice. He warns against attaining a little bit of realization and getting prematurely satisfied and conceited. To the extent that we do so, we tie ourselves up and become unfree.

> NEED I MENTION the Buddha, who was possessed
> of inborn knowledge? — the influence of his six years
> of upright sitting is noticeable still.

"Need I mention the Buddha, who was possessed of inborn knowledge?" He was an exceedingly fine person, born as a prince. Even prior to becoming a monk, he was actually the finest youth in his country, excelling in all kinds of learning, literature, and sports. "The influence of his six years of upright sitting is noticeable still." Even having such extraordinary talents and such a fine character, he still had to struggle for six years. Actually, it was more than that, because for six years prior to beginning his zazen, he practiced the most severe asceticism. Finally he realized that this was not really the way to practice, and started to sit by himself. So even having such tremendous capacity and such an extraordinary personality, still he had to struggle, to go through that much difficulty. So we too should practice hard.

In a way it seems contradictory, for Dōgen Zenji has written that it's not really a matter of practice or enlightenment. If this is true, then why do we have to practice? People often have this kind of question. But again that goes back to the two aspects of our practice. Speaking from the intrinsic perspective, of course, we say that fundamentally we are all buddhas and there is no need for anything such as practice or enlightenment since that is our true nature anyway. But the problem is that we have that perspective only as a theory in which we may believe. We are not aware of it experientially. To become aware of it experientially and know it fully is why we practice.

"Or Bodhidharma's transmission of the mind-seal?" What is the mind-seal? Again it is a synonym for the Way. In a sense, there is nothing to be transmitted. *Realization is itself the transmission.* The teacher just approves it. That is to say, you transmit yourself to yourself. How is it done? Realizing that this very body, this very mind, this very place where we stand is nothing but the Buddha. What more could there be than that? By so doing, you realize that you transmit yourself from yourself, which is nothing but the Buddha. Generation after generation, patriarchs did it. And being approved, it is then handed down. That's why stereotyped, self-styled understanding is insufficient. That's why we emphasize the importance of the transmission by the right teacher who really knows what it is, and how it should be taken care of.

THE FAME OF HIS nine years of wall-sitting is celebrated to this day. Since this was the case with the saints of old, how can men of today dispense with negotiation of the Way?

You should therefore eease from practice based on intellectual understanding, pursuing words and following after speech, and learn the backward step that turns your light inwardly to illuminate your self. Body and mind of themselves will drop away, and your original face will be manifest. If you want to attain suchness, you should practice suchness without delay.

Don't, in other words, be merely involved intellectually and waste your time conceptualizing instead of really practicing. Then your intellectual activities become a kind of obstacle.

"The backward step." This is the key phrase, the key sentence. We always go forward. But instead of going forward, what if we were just to step back and carefully consider how our practice is, how our self is, whether or not we are defiling ourselves? What makes us defiled or stained? That's what Dōgen Zenji points out in the second paragraph. If there is even the slightest discrepancy or difference, that makes the difference of heaven and earth. What makes this discrepancy or gap? Our ego-consciousness.

a-Mo (Bodhidharma), founder of Ch'an, Japanese Sculpture
elson Gallery-Atkins Museum (Nelson Fund)
ansas City, Missouri

By the word "ego" I refer to any consciousness which either divides you or sets you apart from so-called externals. It is this kind of consciousness which discriminates. Of course, the recognition of differences is a very important matter, too. Especially in koan study, you deal with this kind of thing in a very special way. But then you are looking at differences after having realized the oneness. Usually though, dividing ourselves from ourselves or setting ourselves apart from externals, we start creating all kinds of value-judgments such as good, bad, right, wrong. It is, in a way, a necessary matter, and yet because of that we have a problem. So the thing to do is to step backwards and not simply push yourself forward. Then examine and reflect upon yourself carefully, to see how you are dealing with it.

> Body and mind of themselves will drop away, and
> your original face will be manifest.

"Body and mind of themselves will drop away." You don't need to artificially or intellectually concern yourself about it. But when you really practice as I have been describing, it will take care of itself, spontaneously and naturally. So first you sit, then get into samadhi; then, in samadhi, you take care of that limited ego-consciousness. Then you identify with yourself as a whole. It's an almost mechanical process; it just happens in that way.

"Body and mind of themselves will drop away, and your original face will be manifest." See? Original face. Dōgen Zenji even chooses to use this specific kind of phraseology. Definitely he is talking about enlightenment. This "original face" was first mentioned in a koan by the Sixth Patriarch. "If you want to attain suchness, you should practice suchness without delay." Here "suchness" refers to enlightenment. If you want to attain enlightenment, you should practice enlightenment without delay. And the practice of enlightenment is zazen.

> FOR *SANZEN,* a quiet room is suitable. Eat and
> drink moderately. Cast aside all involvements and
> cease all affairs. Do not think good or bad. Do not
> administer pros and cons. Cease all the movements of

the conscious mind, the gauging of all thoughts and views. Have no designs on becoming a buddha. *Sanzen* has nothing whatever to do with sitting or lying down.

At the site of your regular sitting, spread out thick matting and place a cushion above it. Sit either in the full-lotus or half-lotus position. In the full-lotus position, you first place your right foot on your left thigh and your left foot on your right thigh. In the half-lotus, you simply press your left foot against your right thigh. You should have your robes and belt loosely bound and arranged in order. Then place your right hand on your left leg and your left palm facing upwards on your right palm, thumb-tips touching. Thus sit upright in correct bodily posture, neither inclining to the left nor to the right, neither leaning forward nor backward. Be sure your ears are on a plane with your shoulders and your nose in line with your navel. Place your tongue against the front roof of your mouth, with teeth and lips both shut. Your eyes should always remain open, and you should breathe gently through your nose.

Sanzen usually refers to dokusan, which can also be called *nishitsu. Nishitsu* literally means "entering the room", and refers to entering the room of the roshi for private dharma combat and dialogue. But Dōgen Zenji also says that zazen itself is *sanzen.* So here he uses that term as a synonym of zazen, which indicates how important he believes zazen to be. Zazen itself is equal to dokusan or *sanzen.* Of course, from time to time, according to what he is writing about, his emphasis is different, which is quite natural. But since this is instruction on zazen, he gives great emphasis to the importance of sitting itself. And when we really do zazen, that's actually what it's all about.

In *sanzen, san* means "penetration." So the word indicates that you should really penetrate into Zen and really become one with Zen. That is to say, yourself. Then you really become yourself, which is equal to everything. That's *sanzen,* and that's zazen.

When we really get used to sitting, sound as such doesn't bother us so much. But if our zazen is not quite well-matured, being inexperienced, noise bothers us. It's interesting; a constant noise, such as the ticking of a clock, is less disturbing. But music or the human voice are among the worst distractions, since they carry meaning and are constantly changing, and so tend to attract our attention and thus disturb us. A passing car on the street outside is less disturbing, and a constant mechanical noise is still less bothersome. But anyhow, noise tends to disturb us, so a quiet room is preferable.

"Eat and drink moderately." This is very true too. For example, I realize that I tend to eat more than I should, and I also remember how fond Yasutani Roshi was of noodles. Even being more than seventy years of age, Kōryū Roshi can eat quite a lot of noodles, more than I can! So it's kind of hard to really judge; perhaps all of you are eating and drinking more moderately than I do. But moderation is important. And also, it's better to avoid sitting right after eating. Take a good rest, give your stomach a good chance to digest the meal, at least for an hour or so, then start sitting.

"Cast aside all involvements and cease all affairs." You might feel a little awkward about this kind of statement, "casting aside all affairs." How, you might ask, can we participate in ango with all the responsibilities we have to take care of? Not only relating to ango, but also in our personal lives, we have to do all sorts of things too. Some of us have families and households as well. And we get so easily interrupted by these things. But at least when sitting, put aside all these considerations. Sitting and thinking about all sorts of things, one after another, that's not zazen; it's almost like day-dreaming. So when sitting, cast aside all these involvements and affairs; just really try to sit well. Occasionally I say "just sit," but it's a little hard to do so. So you can do it gradually. First try to make yourself empty. Those who are working on koans or on breathing, totally put yourself into your koan or your breathing. Let it occupy you completely. For those who are sitting shikan-taza, it's especially hard at first to "just sit". You are probably not "just sitting," but almost "just thinking," "just imagining," or something else. So in order to avoid that, you can try to cut off all the senses in the following way.

For example, if noise comes to you, instead of placing your-self in opposition to the sound which you are perceiving, and fighting against it, just try to become that sound yourself. Really being that sound yourself, then that sound won't disturb you anymore, because when you really become sound yourself, then the subject involved, the "me", is eliminated. There remains only the sound. And that's the way to empty yourself.

With a koan it's the same process. Really put yourself into the koan, then you'll forget about yourself. That's what we call *ninku,* "man emptied" or "subject emptied". But still there re-mains the dharma, the object. So next, empty that one too. Again, by really being so, you become unaware of even being so. It's a deeper state of samadhi. Then both man and dharma are empty; subject and object are both empty. That stage is called the Great Death. Then when you go that far, just spontaneously it naturally comes out. That's what Dōgen Zenji says: "body and mind spontaneously drop away." In other words, you can tran-scend the bondage of conscious restriction, limitation.

It's not an easy thing to do. So your sitting should be a very solid, powerful thing. And yet you should be free of any physical strain.

> DO NOT THINK good or bad. Do not administer pros
> and cons. Cease all the movements of the conscious
> mind, the gauging of all thoughts and views.

At least when we sit, we shouldn't think. Put thoughts aside. That's what it means. But this doesn't imply that he denies the value of consciousness. He isn't urging us merely to become like dead logs or stones. Without any thoughts or views, our con-sciousness can still clearly function. That's why the surface of the mind is compared to that of a very clear, bright mirror. We cannot say that if there's no reflection, there's no mirror; the mirror is there, and simply reflects whatever is before it. What-ever comes up is clearly shown, and when the object vanishes, so does the reflection. Not a trace remains behind. That's the state of mind we're supposed to maintain during the practice of zazen. But it's hard.

Of course, for those who are working on koans or breathing, this doesn't quite apply. In such cases, you must really be conscious of what you are doing, and try quite hard to concentrate on it. But when you go into samadhi, this happens. Especially for those who are working on shikan-taza, I wish you to encourage yourself to sit like this. I often compare the mind to a pond. When the water is clear and undisturbed, the reflection of the moon overhead is perfectly clear and sharp, and can be seen without any problem. But if the water is muddy and stirred up by winds, it becomes rippled at first, and then even waves arise, and totally obscure and distort the reflections. I think that this analogy is from one of the sutras. And it's certainly true; the mind is always too wavy. Why do we have waves? Because there is wind blowing—the wind of thoughts and opinions and ideas. That is what makes the surface of the mind wavy. If we only had a few ripples, it might not be so bad; at least we could recognize the moon and tell where it is. But when it's really wavy, we cannot even locate the moon, even though it's still reflecting. In other words, we ourselves are nothing but Buddha-nature. We are nothing but mu-ji, Mind, whatever we call it. We cannot recognize it because of that wavy condition. But nonetheless, it is still always reflecting. That is to say, so are we.

So we must make ourselves calm, and then by some chance we may see the reflection of the moon clearly on the surface of the water, and we'll say, "Oh! *This* is it!" And that recognition is always an instantaneous thing; sudden, not gradual. So even if our zazen is very immature, that kind of thing will happen. Of course once it does, if we don't continue to sit, such vision may virtually fade away and disappear, unless it's extremely clear to begin with. And when you have that kind of clarity, then you simply cannot stop practicing.

Samadhi is when you really make your mind calm and still, so that by some chance you can distinctly recognize what the reflection of the moon is, and how it is. In this fashion you realize the true nature, and what it is. That's what Dōgen Zenji says: your original face will manifest. It's almost a mechanical thing.

"Have no designs on becoming a Buddha." If you have any

expectations, then again, right there you have created a split between you and something that you expect. Right there is where dichotomy or dualism comes into being. So when you do zazen, you don't need to expect anything, just do so, just be so.

"*Sanzen* has nothing whatever to do with sitting or lying down." You can appreciate it in two ways: zazen or *sanzen* is not simply regular sitting or lying down. That's one way to appreciate it. And also you might see it as implying that in doing *sanzen,* you must really be constant, from morning to night; whatever you do must be zazen. And that kind of solid, powerful state has nothing to do with regular sitting down or standing up; it deals with the state of *sanzen* in every activity of the day.

The next part is about sitting, and ends with the sentence: "Your eyes should always remain open, and you should breathe gently through your nose." This last sentence is kind of interesting, isn't it? Some teachers place great emphasis on breathing technique, but see how little Dōgen Zenji says about breathing: " . . . you should breathe gently through your nose." This kind of sitting is quite all right. Some of you have had a difficult time of it, concentrating so hard for so long, trying to sit strongly, body erect, trying hard to breathe deeply or slowly. You strain in your physical posture, especially in the stomach or abdominal area, and around the shoulders or chest. During sesshin, generally one or two people will complain of stomach ache or nausea, or tension around the belly area. That's what you should avoid. Those who have difficulty should just breathe, as Dōgen Zenji says, " . . . gently through your nose." But by balancing the body quite nicely, without paying much attention to breathing, you can sit quite well.

I might also mention the disposition of the eyes. First, just gaze straight ahead of yourself, at a point about four feet in front of you, on the floor. For those who sit in smaller rooms, where the walls are closer to you than that, it's very hard on the eyes to sit with them open. And when you focus upon one particular spot, your eyes get tired and you have to adjust the focus. But if there is a clear space in front of you, drop your gaze to the floor. Let your gaze move toward the tip of your nose, and then let it rest upon the floor at a distance of three or four feet.

This is a good eye position, and when you do so, the eyelid naturally moves into a position of half-open, half-shut. Thus without any special effort, you can have proper eye position. But if the wall is really close, and if that makes it hard to sit, you can even close your eyes. In that case, what you have to watch out for is the tendency to become drowsy or to drift into thinking or day-dreaming more readily. So just be aware of that fact and try that much harder to concentrate on whatever it is that you're doing. Thus you can avoid the drowsiness. Of course, it's better to keep the eyes half-opened, but even so, once you've established your practice fairly regularly, you'll not find closed eyes much of a problem. Similarly, once you get used to it, it's not at all difficult to keep the eyes open. I don't want to encourage you to close your eyes, but you can make whatever adjustments of this sort you find most helpful in your sitting.

Dōgen Zenji also speaks about the position of the mouth and tongue. Place the tip of your tongue against the roof of your mouth, so as to make less room for air in the mouth. Close your mouth, sealing it with the lips, so that your teeth are touching. By doing so, practically no air is left in the mouth, and you can decrease your rate of salivation. It's kind of an interesting thing; when you become conscious of your saliva, you tend to produce more of it. But by having this kind of mouth position, you can control it and also strengthen your sitting.

Regarding the body, let me discuss posture briefly. The body should not lean or incline in any direction. Try to sit straight and nicely balanced. Usually I have very poor posture; during the first couple of days of sesshin, my back really aches. But during the third day, my body gets much better, and I can practically cure my own backache, just by sitting!

And even though he doesn't mention arm position, it is still rather important. If you don't have the right arm position, you'll have pain in your shoulder muscles, or they'll get strained. So watch your arm position too. Let your palm be slightly supported by either your leg or your foot. If you have long enough arms, it will rather naturally make a nice circle. I've noticed that some of you position your hands a little too high up on your abdomen. Maybe once you get used to it that position is okay. But the way

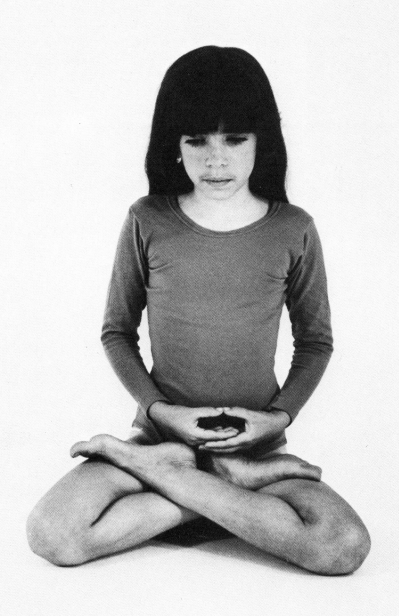

we teach is to let the thumb-tips be about parallel with the navel, with the backs of the hands resting lightly on the soles or heels of the feet. Of course, this only applies to those sitting in the full or half-lotus positions. If you aren't, then just let your hands rest upon your thighs.

Also the lower back is very important. The lower back, the lower abdomen, the joints of the legs, the soles of the feet, and the hands; all these are in the same general area when sitting, and this area forms the very center of your sitting. When you sit you can just about visualize whether you are sitting accurately or not. Even if you suffer from some physical deformity, such as having a crooked back, still it is possible for you to find a position which will permit you to sit quite effectively. Each of us has slight differences in bone and muscle structure, but each of us can adjust his posture accordingly. So please sit strongly. I've heard the term "powerful" used to describe sitting; perhaps that might be a better term to use than "strong". I'm afraid that some people understand the word "strong" to imply a kind of tension. But that's a very bad thing; you can strain yourself to the point of exhaustion. And especially in sesshin, that's not the right way to practice. To sit powerfully requires that your body be free of physical strain or tension. When you really sit powerfully, it's almost as though you were generating electricity; if anybody were to accidentally touch you, sparks would leap out!

When you do shikan-taza, sit as if you were engaged in a duel. In such circumstances, were you to be inattentive, you'd very soon be killed. Being so, what kind of intensity would you have? If you were physically tense, that would greatly interfere with your ability to fight. But in a duel, you must be physically relaxed, and yet have tremendous power of concentration.

Sometimes while sitting, we become drowsy and drift into sleep, or day-dreams. But if we keep that kind of intensity, such drowsiness or scattering of attention immediately goes away and we are able to sit well again.

When you have strong concentration, it also affects the body. If your concentration is strong enough, it can keep you warm, even in the coldest winter weather. The condition of the mind

improves the body. When we feel cold or chilly, the skin gets tighter and the outer air is shut out. And on a hot summer day, the skin opens up and releases the heat of the body. So by train-, ing our consciousness, it is clear that we can, to a certain point, control the body without much difficulty. Even being uncon- scious, the body works that way, so encourage it more con-· sciously, then get better at self-control. For example, when I feel myself coming down with a cold, if I feel, "Oh-oh, I've caught a cold!" then indeed, I get a cold. But if, at that stage, I block it off and decide, "No, I am not going to catch a cold!" then I don't catch cold. It's really interesting, the relationship of body and mind working together. So when you sit, please be attentive to it.

ONCE YOU HAVE adjusted your posture, take a deep breath, inhale and exhale, rock your body right and left and settle into a steady, immobile sitting posi- tion. Think of not-thinking. How do you think of not- thinking? Non-thinking. This in itself is the essential art of zazen.

The zazen I speak of is not learning meditation. It is simply the Dharma-gate of repose and bliss, the practice-realization of totally culminated enlighten- ment. It is the manifestation of ultimate reality. Traps and snares can never reach it. Once its heart is grasped, you are like the dragon when he gains the water, like the tiger when he enters the mountain. For you must know that just there (in zazen) the right Dharma is manifesting itself and that from the first dullness and distraction are struck aside.

When you arise from sitting, move slowly and quietly, calmly and deliberately. Do not rise suddenly or abruptly. In surveying the past we find that trans- cendence of both unenlightenment and enlightenment, and dying while either sitting or standing, have all depended entirely on the strength (of zazen).

"Think of not-thinking. How do you think of not-thinking?

Non-thinking." These are the famous words of Master Yakusan Igen, who is in our lineage. Now a phrase like this could be elaborated quite a bit. But for our purposes, we can plainly take it as, make ourselves unconditioned and just sit. That unconditioned state is a state of non-thinking. Now more directly speaking, what is the unconditioned state? Don't develop or cling to *any* opinionated ideas. Even make yourself very naive. Now in English, "naive" has a rather negative implication or connotation, but in Japanese there is a similar word which has very positive connotations: to make yourself very empty, like clean white paper. Whatever is drawn on it, you can see it very clearly. But if the paper is messed up or something is on it already, whatever you try to put on it then becomes ambiguous and unclear. So in sitting it is very important not to have your own ideas or thinking. That unconditioned, very plain state of mind, that's the state of non-thinking. And with that state of mind, sit. Eliminate all kinds of mental activities, don't even think of becoming Buddha. That's what he means. Even trying to become Buddha or trying to become enlightened becomes a hindrance, because we don't know what enlightenment *is* until we get into that state. So whatever we think of merely becomes an idea. Right there the gap opens up between ourselves and the object we think about. In other words, eliminate that object too. By sitting, concentrating in zazen, we empty ourselves and at the same time we are able to empty the object. So the subject-object relationship is eliminated altogether. Then you become a total being. And that's what he talks about; zazen itself manifests the ultimate reality. That's the kind of zazen he talks about. That's shikan-taza.

So it is not denying the function of our consciousness to say that when we do shikan-taza, we can't think of anything. Consciousness is vividly functioning in the sense of being conditioned by certain ideas or thoughts that we have. If we do that, then right there we find ourselves by those ideas. And that much we restrict ourselves. Actually, this happens all the time. For example, when we have difficulty or problems, we think, "someone is creating the problems for me." But it's not so. If there is any difficulty or problem, it's a problem of our own making.

Always that's the case. It may not seem so but it is. In a narrower sense of the word it is so, and in a broader sense it is so too. Sometimes it is hard to take: for example, if the house next door catches fire, so that the building in which we live is burned out too. We are not doing anything bad, and yet that kind of thing happens. So we can blame others, and yet if we look at it from a larger perspective, they are also part of ourselves. Then actually no one is to blame.

When we really realize what *is* my self, then "my" becomes identical with "your" or "their" or even "its". That is the state of non-thinking. So again, coming back to the point I made at the very beginning, make ourselves plain, as much as possible. Then just be as we are. Then our being becomes an absolute thing.

"Traps and snares can never reach it." What are "traps and snares"? Our ideas, our own thoughts. So that very plain, mirror-like state, that's the state that traps and snares can never reach. That is to say, we trap or snare ourselves. And again it doesn't mean that we deny the significance or importance of mental function. Without that we simply can't survive. But we should try not to have very fixed ideas of our own.

That also reminds me of that statement of Dōgen Zenji in the *Zuimonki* compiled by Master Ejō. It says something like this, "If our teacher says worms and toads are the Buddhas, we'll just simply believe that worms and toads are the Buddhas." That's the way to learn. In other words, make yourself very plain, empty, not having your own opinions. Then you can take whatever is poured in. There is a story in one of the sutras in which a very gullible monk achieved the four stages of arhatship when a senior monk threw a ball at him four times. This simpleton monk simply believed as literally true what the senior monk jokingly told him, and because of his complete faith, he attained enlightenment. It didn't matter that his teacher was not serious. Now *that's* what I call faith.

And exactly the opposite thing can be said. Regardless of how fine a teacher you have, if you cling to something of your own, then that's it. It happened at the time of the Buddha too, when he expounded the *Lotus Sutra*, the *Saddharmapundarika Sutra*, on Mount Grdhakuta. In the beginning of the sutra it says that 500 monks just stood up and left: "The Buddha is talking nonsense, let's leave. . ."

I heard from Yasutani Roshi that Harada Roshi used to explain what the state of shikan-taza is: that is to say, putting yourself into a state of non-thinking, and sitting strong. When we sit, two major types of disturbances may occur. One is *scattered, busy mind,* and another is *dull, drowsy mind.* And the way to eliminate these two while we sit is to concentrate in zazen as though engaged in a life-and-death duel. Unfortunately, we don't sit like that all the time; that much we are untrained.

Q: Roshi, could you say something about how, when you're in that very drowsy condition to begin with, you can more readily get into a strong state?

A: In that case, bring the attention either up to the hairline or to a point between the eyebrows. In other words, doing so, bring up more blood to stimulate the brain, then the drowsiness goes away. The busy mind is the opposite: too much blood going up to the head. Then the head thinks on and on and on, the brain needs more oxygen, and in order to supply more oxygen, more blood goes up. When you have too much blood up in the head, blood circulation gets bad, the head gets heavy, dull, and you may even have a headache. So when we sit, the head should be very light, refreshed. It's like a pyramid. The head is like a point, weightless. Hold nice concentration and balance with your center of gravity in the lower abdomen, then sit like that. Then once you really get into it, it's "like a dragon gaining the water." "Once its heart is grasped, you are like the dragon when he gains the water." It's said that when the dragon gets into the water, it crawls upon the clouds, then ascends into the heavens. "Or like the tiger when he enters the mountain." If a tiger is in the cage in the zoo he is not much, but if he runs freely up in the mountain, we can't even get close. You gain that kind of strength.

THE ZAZEN I SPEAK of is not learning meditation.
It is simply the Dharma-gate of repose and bliss, the
practice-realization of totally culminated enlightenment.

The term used here is "practice-realization" and it's hyphen-
ated. Practice *is* realization itself. Or practicing realization.
Or realization practice. That's our zazen.

Again it reminds me of Yasutani Roshi's comment not only
on zazen, but also on what kind of attitude you should have
toward yourselves. Now most of you have received jukai. It's
a confirmation of one's self. As what? As the Three Treasures.
Now what he says is to have deep faith in the fact that you are
nothing but the Three Treasures. And having that faith, then
sit, work, study. So whatever you do is nothing but the Buddha's
action, expounding and manifesting the Dharma yourselves. And
that is nothing but perfect unity and harmony altogether. Where's
the problem? Even difficulties are nothing but the Dharma itself. What to complain about? What to be frustrated by? What to
be annoyed about? "The practice-realization of totally culminated enlightenment" is "the manifestation of absolute reality."
What is it? In a way it's zazen; and in a way it's yourself. Your
zazen is a total thing, and being so you also become ultimate
and absolute. Now that's the kind of zazen Dōgen Zenji talks
about.

WHEN YOU ARISE from sitting, move slowly and
quietly, calmly and deliberately. Do not rise suddenly
or abruptly. In surveying the past, we find that transcendence of both unenlightenment and enlightenment, and dying while either sitting or standing, have
all depended entirely on the strength (of zazen).

Now actually, this kind of thing happens. You would be amazed
how much we can train ourselves. I think the Third Patriarch,
Kanchi Sōsan Daishi, died standing. Many monks died sitting.
Some even died in a fire, in sitting position. We have a saying,
"Emancipating the mind, even fire becomes cool." It's one of
the lines of poetry one monk composed just before he was

burned up.

And Morita Goryu Roshi, who was the head of Eiheiji five or six generations before me, had to have a tumor removed from his neck, and asked not to have any anaesthetic. The doctor was amazed, but Morita Roshi didn't move once during surgery, or cry out in pain. That's how much you can train yourself. Now that's what Dōgen Zenji mentions here. "Dying while either sitting or standing have all depended entirely on the strength of zazen." He is talking about *jōriki*.

> IN ADDITION, the bringing about of enlightenment by the opportunity provided by a finger, a banner, a needle or a mallet, and the effecting of realization with the aid of a *hossu,* a fist, a staff or a shout, cannot be fully understood by man's discriminitive thinking. Indeed, it cannot be fully known by the practicing or realizing of supernatural powers either. It must be deportment beyond man's hearing and seeing — is it not a principle that is prior to his knowledge and perceptions?

This is the place we get stuck. We try to understand it by our discriminative mind. Somehow we have to start with that discriminative mind, and yet as long as we remain in that domain of consciousness, somehow we can't take care of ourselves well enough to take care of the difficulties and problems we have. I think most of us are really facing this problem. Our discriminative, discursive thought is the very thing that binds us. The question really is: how to go beyond, how to transcend that dichotomy. But we do have to start with that discriminative mind.

These days I have been emphasizing the importance of the aspiration or vow. That is the key. Yesterday I translated an article by Jiun Sonja on the Bodhisattva's Precepts. All of us want to liberate ourselves, to become free and peaceful. But that is not quite enough. That's just the *sravaka* spirit, the spirit of simply wanting one's own salvation. Of course, the *sravaka* spirit could also be interpreted differently, but that's the general idea. But the bodhisattva is something else again.

That is simply to care more about others than about oneself. Since we are altogether one to begin with, regardless of how fully we realize it, it works out beautifully. To think of others first, we do something nice for them; then, in one way or another, sooner or later it benefits ourselves. Dōgen Zenji used to say that only the foolish think that concern for others is at one's own expense. It is not so; benefiting others and oneself is altogether one thing.

I really want you to have strong, inclusive aspiration and vows to accomplish it together. Then with such deep aspiration we encourage our practice. We just keep on going, and deep enlightened experiences will take place in one way or another. Here Dōgen Zenji enumerates examples of such cases.

". . . the bringing about of enlightenment by the opportunity provided by a finger . . ." The finger referred to is, of course, that of Gutei—that famous koan "Gutei's Finger" which appears in the *Gateless Gate* and also in the *Book of Equanimity*. Whatever Gutei was asked, he just stuck up his finger. And when he was dying, he told his disciples, "I got this one-finger Zen from Master Tenryu, and I've used it all my life and have never exhausted it." Then, sticking his finger up, he died.

Each of these objects Dōgen Zenji mentions relates to famous cases of enlightenment: Ananda and the banner in front of the temple; Sekisō's "take a step from the top of a hundred-foot-high pole; Kanadaiba's needle; Manjusri and the mallet; Hyaku-jo and the *hossu;* Basō's shout; Tokusan's staff. All these are actual instances of former patriarchs and bodhisattvas whose enlightenment experiences involved these objects. In each of these instances there is no dichotomy, no room for dichotomy or dualism. No room for thinking. For example, if you burn your finger or you get hurt, there's no room for thinking, you just shriek, "AAARRGGGHH!" That's all. Or being pinched on your nose, you scream. That totalness or absoluteness, that's what you should really experience by yourself. How? Again the same principle, forgetting yourself, really becoming a total being.

"Indeed, it cannot be fully known by the practicing or realizing of supernatural powers either." Some people are attracted by supernatural powers. I've heard that even these days a number of people have certain occult powers. I remember Yasutani Roshi one time telling us that increasing your samadhi power you can really train yourself in that path, you can do that if you wish to. But the point is that even acquiring such supernatural powers won't give us the wisdom by which we liberate ourselves and others from the tie of birth and death. So that is to be our main concern. Every evening we say, "Life and death are of grave importance." To really take care of them or take care of our lives altogether, that is the aim of our practice. So even by having supernatural powers, we cannot fully understand what the enlightened state is.

THIS BEING the case, intelligence or lack of it does not matter; between the dull and the sharp-witted there is no distinction.

This reminds me, from time to time these days I have been paying more attention and being careful about how I express myself in terms of women's practice. Some call me a male chauvinist. I don't particularly think I am so, but I might have given such an impression to some of you. But as far as this kind of awareness or realization is concerned, there's no distinction. Regardless of being male or female, we have the same opportunity, same chance, and it all depends on us. In Kōryū Roshi's place there is an exceedingly well-accomplished woman. I think she is still alive, though over eighty, and is just an exquisite lady. I heard that she studied and finished koan study with Harada Roshi and that after that she studied and also finished koan study with Kōryū Roshi! So similarly in this country among you, that kind of person will hopefully come out. It's not a matter of any distinction whatsoever.

IF YOU CONCENTRATE your effort single-mindedly, that in itself is negotiating the Way. Practice-realization is naturally undefiled.

What makes defilement are self-centered, ego-centered ideas. All of us are using wisdom. That's what Buddha says too. We are using it constantly. When the time comes, we get up; when the time comes, we eat. Everything goes smoothly, it's wisdom. Not only for the human, but for everything else. But somehow or other we all mix it up, and don't do it. Ideally, whatever comes along, day after day, we just put ourselves into it.

Then "practice-realization is naturally undefiled. Going forward in practice is a matter of everydayness." This is one of the most important statements in this *Fukanzazengi*, "going forward is a matter of everydayness." Going forward regardless of how far we achieve or we accomplish, still it's ordinary. Regardless of how far we go, still it's everyday. "Everyday" sounds a little awkward. I noticed a couple of other places where it was a little awkward, at least I felt awkward. Somehow I like that word "ordinary." I was very impressed when I was told the etymological implication of "ordinary." *Ord* derives from "order." I think it's originally Latin. Orderliness is extremely important. Orderliness of mind, orderliness of body, orderliness of daily life, orderliness of even the moon, surroundings, orderliness of groups, orderliness of society, country, everything. That's supposed to be ordinary. Then it's no problem. No matter how far we go, we are just whatever we are. Got to be. So we don't need to lose our heads, or put an extra head on top of ours. Ordinary. If we can live everyday like that, it will be no problem. Then practice-realization is naturally undefiled.

IN GENERAL, this world and other worlds as well, both in India and China, equally hold the Buddha-seal, and over all prevails the character of this school, which is simply devotion to sitting, total engagement in immobile sitting. Although it is said that there are as many minds as there are men, still they all negotiate the Way solely in zazen. Why leave behind the seat that exists in your home and go aimlessly off to the dusty realms of other lands? If you make one misstep you go astray from the Way directly before you.

Now again in these passages we see Dōgen Zenji's strong emphasis on zazen. "This world and other worlds as well, both in

India and China." It says China, but Korea and Japan are included in this talk, all the Eastern lands. "This world" is the world where Shakyamuni resides, and the other world, the Western world, is the world of Amida Buddha, and the Eastern world is Yakushi Nyorai's realm. Each direction of the compass is governed by different Tathagathas. Yasutani Roshi used to say, thousands of Buddhas are living, taking care of us and of everything else. How do we relate to them?

He talks about the "Buddha-seal". What is the Buddha-seal? It is nothing but our lives and awareness and wisdom, the transmitted understanding about our lives which is the "character of this school." It all depends on our devoting ourselves to sitting, "total engagement in immobile sitting." Nothing but zazen. Although whatever we want to do is hindered by zazen, we can't help but do zazen. This is true. If all of us were to sit like that, to attain enlightenment, as Dōgen Zenji says, would be as simple as eating three meals a day. But since we don't do it, it won't happen. Reflecting upon myself, I feel that I should sit much, much more. When I have to do something and can't sit, it's almost like an excuse. So at least when we sit, we try to really sit well, like immobile mountains.

"Although it is said that there are as many minds as there are men, still they negotiate the Way solely in zazen." Although each of us is different, how we understand is different and what we have learned is different, yet we should practice *sanzen bendō*. *Sanzen:* "penetrating in Zen, or doing zazen." *Bendō:* "to accomplish the Way." We should practice *sanzen bendō*, "penetrating in zazen, accomplishing the Way."

"Why leave behind the seat that exists in your home and go aimlessly off to the dusty realms of other lands?" Now when we read this line, we might have the first impression that he is talking about going from here to someplace else, for example to China or Japan, to practice. Of course in a sense it has that implication, but there is another implication too. "Dusty realms." Sometimes the objects of our senses are called the "six dusts". In other words, when we are conditioned by what we see, hear, smell, taste, think and feel, they become dust. So instead of being in the conditioned state, we take the initiative to control or adjust. There is a famous expression by Master Rinzai: "You be-come a master wherever you are or whatever you do. Then everyplace, whatever you do, everything becomes true." And vice-versa, if we are controlled by what we perceive or conceive, we become like a servant or a slave. That's the dust he's talking about.

And what is the "seat"? It's a diamond seat, the lion seat where the Buddha sits. That's supposed to be our zazen. The very zafu on which we sit is the seat of the diamond and the seat of the Buddha; so we don't need to go anyplace but right here. We stand, we sit on the seat of the Tathagatha.

"If you make one misstep you go astray from the Way directly before you." That reminds me of the well-known analogy in the *Lotus Sutra* of the beggar who is the long-lost son of a million-aire. Wandering around all his life thinking himself a beggar, he finally ends up at his father's house. His father recognizes him immediately, but not until the son is accustomed to the wealth that is actually his all along does his father reveal himself and leave him his possessions. So "if you make one misstep, you go astray from the Way directly before you."

"You have gained the pivotal opportunity of human form." It's so true, though: how precious and how rare it is to be born as a human. Usually we don't pay much attention to this. Even just around the Center we have countless life-forms. Even in that sink in the backyard, how many lives are living there: bacteria, algae, tadpoles, birds, flies flying around. To be human is really a precious thing. Being human, right there we are able to be Tathagathas.

YOU HAVE GAINED the pivotal opportunity of human form. Do not use your time in vain. You are maintaining the essential working of the Buddha-way. Who would take wasteful delight in the spark from the flintstone? Besides, form and substance are like the dew on the grass, destiny like the dart of lightning— emptied in an instant, vanished in a flash.

In the concluding passage of the *Diamond Sutra* it says, "our body is like dew or like a fountain, like a dream or like a flash of lightning, emptied in an instant, vanished in a flash." Now in a way, life is long, between seventy and a hundred years nowadays. But when we compare it to infinite time, it's a short time indeed. And again, the time we can really put into our practice is also very limited. So the time we have right now is really precious time. Let us reflect upon ourselves, how we can have a stronger, better practice together. And not only make ourselves happy and content, but share such understanding, freedom and peace with other people.

PLEASE, HONORED followers of Zen. Long accustomed to groping for the elephant, do not be suspicious of the true dragon. Devote your energies to a way that directly indicates the absolute. Revere the man of complete attainment who is beyond all human agency. Gain accord with the enlightenment of the buddhas; succeed to the legitimate lineage of the patriarchs' samadhi. Constantly perform in such a manner and you are assured of being a person such as they. Your treasure-store will open of itself, and you will use it at will.

In this last paragraph he sums up again what zazen is and what it does for us. The passage, "Long accustomed to groping . . ." refers to the parable of the blind men and the elephant, in which a group of blind men try to find out what an elephant is like, using only their sense of touch. One, feeling the trunk, says that elephants are shaped like snakes; another, feeling the legs, says that elephants are like trees; each blind man clings to his limited perception, and so jumps to a false conclusion.

In the same way we have our own stylized ideas, understandings and concepts, and then we stick to them and regard them as measurements. To that extent we can't accept anything else. Definitely, a larger container can contain more, and our practice is to become bottomless. How to become bottomless? —forgetting one's self. To study the Buddha Way, to transmit the samadhi of the patriarchs, we've got to be bottomless. Otherwise it won't go in. That's what he talks about here.

"Do not be suspicious of the true dragon." What does the true dragon stand for? Freedom. Be free to be yourself. Whatever we attach to, by that we are bound, even by enlightenment. We can be bound by enlightenment, by freedom, even by peace, in which case, of course, there is actually no enlightenment, freedom, or peace. Similarly, if, like the blind men, we get attached to our limited perceptions of the elephant (life), we miss the true dragon, which is life as it really is. That's one interpretation of this passage.

Then there's another interpretation. The line goes: being accustomed to the imitation, then "don't be suspicious of the true dragon." This "true dragon," by the way, is still another story. There was a man by the name of Shoko, who loved dragons. And all over his room, there were pictures of dragons, and sculptures of dragons, and ceramics, all kinds of dragons, and he loved them. So the true dragon up in heaven was very impressed and appreciated it, and one day he wanted to visit Shoko and show him the true dragon. So one night he came down to visit Shoko and stuck his face in through one window and his tail in through the other window, and Shoko was so shocked that he fainted.

Enjoying the imitation, don't miss the real, don't be suspicious about the real. As an interpretation I sense the latter one would be more adequate in this case: long accustomed to imitations, do not be suspicious of the true.

"Devote your energies to a way that directly indicates the absolute." That is zazen. That's what you are doing. "Revere the man of complete attainment who is beyond all human agency." That's kind of hard to translate again. I'm not particularly in favor of this translation. Revere the man who is *zetsu gaku mui*—this is a kind of idiomatic expression. *Zetsu gaku* means "stopped learning." In other words, nothing to learn anymore. Sometimes we say "no-learning." Like "ten no-learnings." Adding two to the Eightfold Path, a ninth one, "right wisdom," and the last one, "right liberation," we get ten "no-learnings." That's *zetsu gaku.* Being liberated, nothing to learn anymore. And *mui* means "non-doing, doing nothing." Not doing nothing physically, though: doing anything, everything, whatever's necessary, yet not doing it. In other words, totally absorbed by whatever you are doing.

Dōgen Zenji says that when you meet the person who expounds the Dharma, don't think of the caste that person came from, don't think of the appearance, either good-looking or bad-looking. Don't think of conduct or behavior. Don't be bothered by that kind of thing. But because of paying reverence to the prajna wisdom, every day, day after day, make three bows to him three times daily. That means at least nine times. Don't raise any frustrations or complications, agitations within yourself. Making yourself empty, unconditioned as much as possible, listen carefully. Then whatever he says comes in without any friction. "Revere the man of complete attainment who is beyond all human agency." The man of complete attainment is always in the midst of all human agency, and goes with it without disturbance or friction. Otherwise, what is the use?

"Gain accord with the enlightenment of the Buddhas." "Gain" —this is again not quite adequate. The word *gattō* means "to become one, to make one." So make ourselves one with the bodhi of the Buddhas. In other words, we become the Buddha ourselves. "Succeed to the legitimate lineage of the Patriarchs' samadhi." He is talking about zazen, really do sit and become zazen yourself. As I say, you are not doing zazen, but zazen is doing zazen. That's what samadhi is. And when you get into that samadhi, right there the legitimate lineage of the Patriarchs is manifested, is succeeded. "Constantly perform in such a manner and you are assured of being a person such as they." If you do "this," this suchness, that's *immo*. *Immo* is also the equivalent of enlightenment.

Then if we read again, there is a matter of interpretation. When we read it as "constantly perform in such a manner," it becomes a kind of conditional, "if you do such-and-such, then such-and-such." That's the way it's usually translated. But instead of reading "if you do such and such," we can read it "since it is this suchness." Already it's almost like a present perfect tense. "Since it is already this, just do it in that way, or just be that." And when we really do that, the treasure-store, the treasure-house opens by itself. And then we can use that treasure as we wish. In fact that's what we are doing. It's not a matter of something happening in the future, but it's always right now, right here.

It's as though I owned a fine house, which had been overrun and occupied by a bunch of rowdy strangers and filled full of trash and garbage. Even though it is my house, I can't use it. So make that house empty first, evacuate it, then afterwards you can use it as your own. See, we have our own head; then we have to make it usable, available for ourselves. So in order to do so, do zazen and clear it up. Dōgen Zenji doesn't say that, though, in the *Fukanzazengi*. But we can interpret it something like that, to forget the self. To forget the self is to really clean up the treasure house. Inexhaustible treasures, abundant treasures, not junk. By cleaning up, we can appreciate them. It's a treasure of formless form, not limited, not restricted, to any extent. Then we can use them, we can appreciate them as we wish. That's the conclusion of this *Fukanzazengi*. "Your treasure store will open of itself and you will use it at will." Again, it goes back to the very beginning. "The Way is perfect and all-pervading." That Way is the treasure-house. And the Dharma-vehicle is free and untrammelled. That Dharma-wheel, Dharma-vehicle, that's the treasure-house. It's nothing but ourselves. So please appreciate yourself. And don't let your treasure-house be occupied by hungry ghosts and fighting spirits, but by buddhas and patriarchs and bodhisattvas. Let's share that treasure together.

CHAPTER 4
Notes on Gassho and Bowing
Taizan Maezumi Roshi
with John Daishin Buksbazen

VISITORS to the Zen Center often ask about the gassho and about bowing. What, they inquire, is the meaning of these gestures? Why are they done? And why is it necessary to do them so precisely and uniformly? These questions deserve careful consideration.

Although we are Zen Buddhists, it should be noted that the gassho and the bow are common to all sects of Buddhism, both Mahayana and Theravada. These two gestures date from the earliest days of Buddhism, or even earlier than that, and they have moved from India throughout the Orient, finally arriving recently in the Western world.

When Shakyamuni Buddha's enlightenment occurred, he went to see five of his former comrades with whom he had practiced various austerities and spiritual disciplines prior to his enlightenment. These five men, who were very devout monks, felt that their companion had gone astray when he abandoned their customary practices. "Come," they said to each other, "Let's not pay any attention to poor Gautama, he no longer is one of us."

They were dismayed to find that he had seemingly stopped his spiritual practices, going so far as to even drink milk and take a bath (two forbidden acts according to their tradition). They could not understand why he seemed only to sit quietly, doing nothing of any value.

But when the Buddha approached them, it is reported that these five monks were so struck by the transformation of their former friend, by his serenity and the radiance of his personality, that they spontaneously placed their palms together and greeted him with deep bows. Perhaps it is a little misleading to say that they greeted *him*. More accurately, it should be said that they were bowing not to their old friend Gautama, but rather to the Buddha—the Enlightened One.

What the Buddha had experienced was the Supreme Great Enlightenment (in Sanskrit, *anuttara samyak sambodhi):* the direct and conscious realization of the oneness of the whole universe, and of his own unity with all things. This is what enlightenment means. This very realization is actually in itself the act of being the Buddha. And it was to this enlightened state that the five monks bowed.

When the Buddha was enlightened, the first thing he said was: "Wonder of wonders! All sentient beings have this same (enlightened) nature!" What this implies is that in bowing to the Buddha, the monks were actually bowing to themselves, and to all beings. These monks were recognizing the great unity which their former companion had directly and profoundly experienced.

Let us examine the gassho and the bow more closely.

GASSHO:

The word *gassho* literally means "to place the two palms together". Of all the mudras (symbolic hand-gestures or positions) we use, it is perhaps the most fundamental, for it arises directly from the depths of enlightenment. Its uses are many, but most commonly it is employed to express respect, to prevent scattering of the mind, to unify all polarities (such as left and right, passive and dominant, etc.) and to express the One Mind—the total unity of Being.

Although there are many types of gassho, in the Soto sect we are primarily concerned with these four:

1. *The Firm Gassho.* The most formal of the gasshos, this is the one most commonly used in our daily practice. It is the gassho we use upon entering the zendo, and upon taking our seats. We also use it at least sixteen times in the course of a formal meal, and during all services. It is made by placing the hands together, palm to palm in front of the face. The fingers are placed together, and are straight rather than bent, while the palms are slightly pressed together so that they meet. The elbows are held somewhat out from the body, although the forearms are not quite parallel with the floor. There is about one fist's distance between the tip of the nose and the hands. Fingertips are at about the same height from the floor as the top of the nose. This gassho has the effect of helping to establish an alert and reverential state of mind.

2. *The Gassho of No-Mind.* This is the next most commonly used gassho. It is basically used in greeting one another or our teachers. In this position, the hands are held a little more loosely together, with a slight space between the palms, although the fingers still touch. The elevation of the elbows from the floor is not so great as in the Firm Gassho; forearms should be at approximately a 45-degree angle to the floor. This gassho has the effect of deepening one's state of samadhi.

3. *The Lotus Gassho.* This gassho is used primarily by officiating priests on special ceremonial occasions. It is made like the *gassho of no-mind,* except that the tips of the middle fingers are held one inch apart. Its name derives from the resemblance of this hand position to the shape of a just-opening lotus bud.

4. *The Diamond Gassho.* This gassho is also known as the *gasshō of being one with life.* Like the *lotus gasshō,* it is used by officiants in services. Although

the hands and arms are in basically the same position as in the *gassho of no-mind,* the *diamond gassho* is made with the fingers of each hand extended and interlocking, and with the right thumb on top of the left.

In each of these gasshos, we keep the eyes focused upon the tips of our middle fingers. But regardless of the style or variety of the gassho, and in whatever setting it is used, the fundamental point of the gassho is to be one with the Three Treasures: Buddha, Dharma, and Sangha.

Of course, we can look at the Three Treasures from many perspectives, and with varying degrees of depth and clarity. At perhaps the most superficial level, the Three Treasures are seen as external objects of supreme reverence for all Buddhists. Unfortunately, in this view, the Three Treasures tend to be perceived as something other than oneself. But as our vision opens up, we experience that each of us is, in fact, the Buddha. We see clearly that everything we encounter in the world is none other than the Dharma—the functioning of underlying enlightenment. And, realizing the oneness of all beings, we come to realize that the Sangha—the all-embracing brotherhood of practice—is simply all composite things, including each of us. Having this awareness we become—or rather, we *are*—one with the Three Treasures.

So, joining our hands palm to palm, we simultaneously create and express the absolute, the oneness which goes beyond all dichotomies. It is from this perspective that we make the gassho, and that we bow.

It is no ordinary person who bows; it is the Three Treasures recognizing itself in all things. If anyone thinks of himself as "just ordinary", he is, in effect, defaming the Three Treasures. And as we place our palms together we unite wisdom and samadhi, knowledge and truth, enlightenment and delusion.

BOWING:

Dōgen Zenji once said: "As long as there is true bowing, the Buddha Way will not deteriorate." In bowing, we totally pay respect to the all-pervading virtue of wisdom, which is the Buddha.

In making the bow, we should move neither hastily nor sluggishly but simply maintain a reverent mind and humble attitude. When we bow too fast, the bow is then too casual a thing; perhaps we are even hurrying to get it over and done with. This is frequently the result of a lack of reverence.

On the other hand, if our bow is too slow, then it becomes a rather pompous display; we may have gotten too attached to the feeling of bowing, or our own (real or imagined) gracefulness of movement. This is to have lost the humble attitude which a true bow requires.

When we bow, it is always accompanied by gassho, although the gassho itself may not always be accompanied by bowing. As with the gassho, there are numerous varieties and styles of bowing, but here we will deal only with the two main kinds of bow which we use in our daily practice.

1. *The Standing Bow.* This bow is used upon entering the zendo, and in greeting one another and our teachers. The body is erect, with the weight distribution evenly and the feet parallel to each other. The appropriate gassho is made (see above). As the bow is made, the body bends at the waist, so that the torso forms an angle with the legs of approximately 45 degrees. The hands (in gassho) do not move relative to the face, but remain in position and move only with the whole body.

2. *The Deep Bow (Full Prostration).* This bow is most often used at the beginning and end of services, and upon entering and leaving dokusan. It is somewhat more formal than the standing bow, and requires a continuous concentration during its execution so that it is not sloppily done.

   The bow itself begins in the same way as the *standing bow,* but once the body is bent slightly from the waist, the knees bend and one assumes a kneeling position. From the kneeling position, the movement of the torso continues, with the hands separating and moving, palms upward, into a position parallel with the forehead. As the bowing movement progresses, the backs of the hands come to rest just above the floor and the forehead is lowered until it rests upon the floor between the hands. At this point, the body is touching the floor at knees, elbows, hands, and forehead. The hands are then slowly raised, palms upward, to a point just above the ears. Then the hands slowly return to the floor. This action is a symbolic placing of the Buddha's feet above one's head as an act of reverence and humility. There should be no sharp, abrupt movements of the hands or arms, no bending of the wrists or curling of the fingers while executing this gesture. When the hands have been raised and lowered, the body then straightens as the person bowing gets to his feet once again and ends in gassho, just as he began. In kneeling, actually the knees do not touch the ground simultaneously, but in sequence; first, the right and then the left knee touches the ground. The same is true for the right and left hands and right and left elbows, in that sequence. In practice, however, the interval between right and left sides touching the ground may be so minute as to be unnoticeable. In bowing, movement should not be jerky or disjointed, but should flow smoothly and continuously without either disruption or arrested motion.

Master Ōbaku, the teacher of Master Rinzai, was famous for his frequent admonition to his students. "Don't expect anything from the Three Treasures." Time after time he was heard to say this. One day, however, Master Ōbaku was observed in the act of bowing, and was challenged about his practice.

"You always tell your students not to expect anything from the Three Treasures," said his questioner, "and yet you have been making deep bows." In fact, he had been bowing so frequently for so long that a large callus had formed on his forehead at the point where it touched the hard floor. When asked how he explained this, Master Ōbaku replied, "I don't expect. I just bow."

This is the state of being one with the Three Treasures. Let us just make gassho. Let us just bow.

CHAPTER 5
Breathing in Zazen
Kōryū Ōsaka Roshi

I SHOULD like to talk briefly about breathing. To begin with I should like you to have a natural kind of breathing, based on your natural breathing cycle, and try to improve or develop it. Generally speaking, the normal frequency of our breaths is roughly 17 times per minute. For those who are more experienced in sitting the frequency of breathing per minute decreases, becoming 5 to 6 times per minute, 2 to 3 times per minute, or even less. However, if you try to slow your breath artificially, then your breathing becomes very awkward and your sitting becomes very uncomfortable. So in order to improve your breathing, try to narrow your breathing. It's sort of hard to explain, but for example, when you exhale, exhale less than you usually do each moment so that less air is exhaled. Do not try to lengthen the span of your breathing immediately, but just try to exhale a smaller amount. Narrow the stream of air, then breathe with your normal frequency. When you inhale, do not inhale too much air at one time, but try to inhale a smaller amount. Again, do not lengthen the span of breathing right away. By breathing like this, more air is saved in the lungs, making it easier for you to breathe. As a quite natural consequence your breathing will slow down.

If you breathe like this, since you have more air in your lungs you can breathe more comfortably. Being comfortable, you can sit better, and sitting better, your breathing becomes slower. Then not only does your breathing become slower, but deeper too. And when you try to breathe like this, eventually you start to experience the very subtle taste of breathing.

When you breathe, not only to make your breath longer and deeper, but also to smooth the transition from inhalation to exhalation, your breathing becomes somewhat like the shape of an egg, an oval cycle, very smoothly circulating the breath. When you practice this kind of breathing your sitting becomes really good and you even have joy, an almost immeasurable pleasure, to simply breathe in zazen.

In order to breathe from the lower abdomen, some of you sort of push it down; that is the wrong way. Instead of trying to push the air down, rather try to push your lower abdomen forward slightly as you inhale, then as you exhale, the lower abdomen goes in. When you inhale, it goes out; when you exhale it goes in. If you try to push the air down, then you compress the diaphragm and also the stomach area, and you may start having pain or unpleasant tension, strain in that area, which should not be. Eventually you can acquire the deep, quiet, natural breathing in your lower abdomen.

As I have explained, please try to breathe in such a way; make your breathing narrower, breathe more slowly in and out, and by doing so your breath very naturally becomes longer.

When you sit, your breath and body and mind become harmonized, and when your breath slows down, the mind also calms down. So try to have this unified, comfortable feeling when you do zazen, and please do not be hasty. You have to acquire this by yourself regardless of what kind of talks you listen to or hear, and if you don't practice it, it is no good. From individual to individual it won't happen in exactly the same way. Each of you has to find out the suitable, comfortable way to achieve this unified, harmonized condition of breathing, body, and mind. This is the very fundamental condition for practicing

Zen. Please do not be hasty, but diligently acquire this kind of breathing.

When you count the breath, there are different ways to count, such as when you exhale, count "one", and sustain that number when you inhale. Then the opposite way, when you inhale count "one", and when you exhale count "two". But the most commonly practiced one is when you exhale, start counting "one" and continue that number while you inhale, then when you exhale again, count "two".

At any rate, when you begin the practice of following the breath, try to really become one with breathing; when you exhale, try to really become one with exhalation...

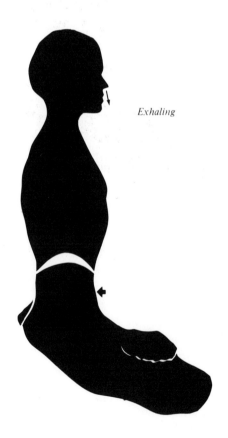

Exhaling

Inhaling

...and when you inhale, again, try to become one with the inhalation. Please, try, and feel the very pleasant, deep feeling of joy in sitting.

CHAPTER 6
Koan Practice and Shikan-taza
Hakuun Yasutani Roshi

IF we were to distinguish the various kinds of Zen now practiced in Japan, we would find two major types: koan Zen and shikan-taza. The Rinzai and Ōbaku Schools emphasize koan study; the Soto School emphasizes shikan-taza. But even when koan study is stressed shikan-taza is not abandoned. The great masters of these three schools always emphasized the importance of shikan-taza. Conversely, the finest masters always used koans freely.

Dōgen Zenji, who brought Soto Zen to Japan, was instrumental in bringing his first disciple, Ejō Zenji, to enlightenment by giving him the koan, "One thread going through many holes". Since then, many masters of the Soto School have guided their students with koans. Although those who do not have clear vision or wisdom often tend to disparage koan study, there are still Soto masters whose Dharma-eye is clear.

When you study koans, you should not study by yourself; you may fall into traps or go in the wrong direction. You must work under the right teacher. Even if you read a great deal, it is wise to keep in mind that books without a teacher are inadequate guides.

Koans reveal the very essence of the Buddha way, uninterruptedly transmitted to us from the time of Shakyamuni Buddha. After the Sixth Patriarch, Hui-neng, especially in the Sung dynasty and in the following years, koan Zen became very popular in China, and was then carried over into Japan.

Koans

The word "koan" originally meant a public document of great authority issued by the government. In present day usage the word "koan" retains its original implication of authority and rightness. It is by means of the koan that we examine the most fundamental and important problems, or questions, of life—such questions as: What is life? What is death?

Many koans consist of dialogues between Zen masters and their students. Others are often taken from important passages of Buddhist scripture. Among the koans of dialogue, there are some in which the student questions the master in order to clarify his understanding of Buddhism. In others, we see that although the student has experienced enlightenment, his vision is not yet quite clear. In order to clarify and deepen his vision the student visits various masters. In yet another kind of koan, monks or priests who have already had a clear enlightenment experience further train themselves by visiting a number of masters and having Dharma combat with them. The custom of studying under various masters and engaging them in Dharma combat helps the priests or monks (or laymen) to become better teachers themselves.

A koan is not an explanation or illustration of a thought or an idea. If you regard a koan in this way, you lose its real meaning.

Koans deal with the essence of the Dharma, with the realization that all sentient beings are the Buddha. And this fact is the ground of our being. In other words, we use the koan as an expedient means to perceive and demonstrate our Buddhahood, which, in essence, is inexpressible.

Shikan-taza

Needless to say shikan-taza should be personally and individually taught by the right teacher. To practice shikan-taza by yourself, in accordance with nothing more than written instructions, is less harmful than unsupervised koan study, but the proper instructions are very rare. The *Fukanzazengi* by Dōgen Zenji is good instruction, but is very difficult for beginners to understand. It is especially hard to comprehend how to control and adjust the condition of mind, and how the practice should be related to enlightenment as such, so here I will briefly explain how to practice shikan-taza.

Generally speaking, zazen is to be described in three phases: first, adjusting the body; second, adjusting the breathing; and third, adjusting the mind. The first and second are the same in both koan Zen and shikan-taza. However, in the third, adjusting the mind, there is a big difference.

In order to do shikan-taza, first of all it is very important to have a firm faith or belief. Just as in koan study it is generally very important to have questioning, so in the practice of shikan-taza faith is required; faith in the fact that all sentient beings are originally Buddhas. Dōgen Zenji says in the ninth chapter of *Gakudō Yōjinshū (Precautions on Learning the Way):*

> "You should practice along *with* the way. Those who believe in the Buddha-way must believe in the fact that their own self is in the midst of the Way from the beginning, so that there is no confusion, no delusion, no distorted viewpoint, no increase or decrease, and no errors. To have such faith and to understand such a way and practice in accordance with it, is the very fundamental aspect of the learning of the Way. You try to cut off the root of consciousness by sitting. Eight, even nine out of ten will be able to see the Way —have kensho—suddenly."

This is the key to practicing shikan-taza. This does not at all mean that one must believe that the small-minded, egocentric life is no other than the Buddha's. On the contrary, casting all sorts of self-consciousness away and making yourself unconditioned as if a sheet of plain white paper, sit; just firmly sit. Sit with no conditioning, believing in the fact that such sitting itself is nothing but the actualization of Buddhahood which is the same as that of Shakyamuni Buddha or Bodhidharma. This is the very foundation of shikan-taza. If one's faith in that fact is weak, his shikan-taza also becomes weak and becomes less effective.

The next important aspect of doing shikan-taza is to maintain that tension or alertness of the mind, especially for beginners (those who have been practicing 5 to 10 years could be called beginners). It is a common phenomenon that due to weakened or loosened concentration, either one becomes self-conscious or falls into a sort of trance or ecstatic state of mind. Such practice might be useful to relax yourself; however, it will never be the practice of the Buddha-way.

When you thoroughly practice shikan-taza, even in the winter you will sweat. Such extreme tension of the mind cannot be maintained for long periods of time. You might think that you can, but this tension will naturally loosen. So sit half an hour, less than an hour, then stand up and do kinhin. During kinhin, loosen such extreme tension and concentration of the mind. Then refresh yourself and continue to do shikan-taza. To do shikan-taza does not mean to become thoughtless. Such practice is the practice of Hinayana Zen, not that of Mahayana Zen. Yet, in a state of shikan-taza, you cannot have thoughts such as wishing to have enlightenment, or thinking about what an enlightened state might be like, or imagining what is the Buddha. Such a state of mind should not arise in shikan-taza, Dōgen Zenji says: "Do not attempt to become Buddha". So just sit with such extreme concentration, patience, and alertness, that if someone absent-mindedly touches you while you are sitting, it causes a spark to leap. When you continue such sitting, very naturally you return to the original Buddha, which is the very nature of yourself. Then, by almost any chance occurrence, you can be plunged into the sudden realization that all sentient beings are originally Buddhas and all existence is perfect from the beginning, and absolute.

This sort of experience, this awareness, is called satori. One must have this sudden experience. You know that when a bomb explodes, it blows things up. Regardless of how well you know bombs and the theory of explosions, without an actual explosion nothing will be blown up. In the same manner, no matter how well you know about satori or enlightenment, until you actually have satori by yourself, you cannot be with it, you will not be aware of yourself as Buddha.

In short, shikan-taza is the actual practice of Buddhahood itself from the very beginning, so that when the time comes, one will become aware of that very fact.

In the olden days, at all times they practiced zazen in this way. However, to practice in this manner requires a long time to attain enlightenment because such practice should never be discontinued until one becomes completely enlightened. Even after attaining great enlightenment and receiving *inka* from one's master, one must continue to do shikan-taza forever, simply because shikan-taza is not some sort of method of attaining enlightenment or satori, but rather, it is the actualization of satori itself.

CHAPTER 7
Shikan-taza and Koan Practice
Kōryū Ōsaka Roshi

WHAT is satori, and what kind of relationship does it have with the koan?

A: Buddhism is the teaching of the Buddha. The original meaning of the Sanskrit term "Buddha" is "The Awakened One". Thus the term "Buddha" in itself implies that it is the way of awakening oneself, and of helping others to awaken. It is the way of self becoming aware of self; of penetrating the life of the universe, making it one's own life; and of living totally as one with it.

Dōgen Zenji says, "To study Buddhism is to study the self, to study the self is to forget the self, to forget the self is to be enlightened by all things. It is to be liberated from the body and mind of oneself and of the self of others." Therefore, one who wishes to seek enlightenment must start by studying himself. It is very important to keep the body and mind healthy and to unite them harmoniously. Centering around the lower abdomen *(tanden* and *kikai)*, physical, mental, and spiritual power become harmonious and consequently the limitless power of concentration and of samadhi is increased. As a result, unthinkable sudden leaps will occur, and prajna wisdom will be realized. This is called *kanshō hannya* ("illuminating wisdom") and in Zen, this is called kensho and it is satori.

The *Heart Sutra* is the sutra in which enlightenment is explained. It begins: "Avalokitesvara Bodhisattva, doing deep Prajna Paramita, clearly saw Mu of all the five conditions, thus redeeming misfortune and pain." Avalokitesvara Bodhisattva is nothing but the state of enlightenment we attain when we become a Bodhisattva. Attaining enlightenment, we obtain satori as I will explain in the following passages.

Satori means that the body and mind of an individual are unified, and further, that no ego, no mind, no thoughts, and no ideas are recognized. Beyond this, he makes yet one more leap and is reborn as his own true self, identifying himself with the universe. In Zen, this state is called "the great rebirth after the great death." And to live after death is the way of Zen.

The Sutra says in the next phrase, "All five conditions are empty". The five conditions, *shiki ju sō gyō shiki,* mean the human body and mind. The emptiness of both body and mind means to be in the state of no-self or no-mind. In actual Zen practice, it is a state which is experienced as: "Above the cushion there is no man, and under the cushion there is no floor." When you experience this sort of realization of yourself, all sorts of physical problems disappear, and all sorts of tension and rigidity in the mind are dissolved. That is why we say that it redeems all sorts of sufferings. There the true satori lies, and there is a life of infinity, unrestricted by either time or space. This is the life of one who identifies himself with the Buddha, and where such a one stands is the Pure Land of Mind. When you realize this satori, you will be able to live in an eternal moment, and there you find delight and the significance of life.

The koan is a very effective and appropriate means by which to enter into this state. For example, there is Jōshū's "mu"; since it is only one word, it can facilitate realization of the oneness of the subject-object relationship more effectively than by other means such as the *nembutsu* prayer. This holds true whether one works on mu-ji in the attitude of having great faith or intense questioning. The realization of satori is possible in either way. We have many koans, so that you can select a koan which most closely suits your practice. It is important, however, to begin koan practice by working on a koan of the *Hosshin* category. The *Hosshin* koans are those koans by which one realizes the Dharmakaya. That is to say, that this flesh-and-blood body itself is simultaneously infinite and indestructible. The *Hosshin* koans are those which make individuals realize that this limitless and unrestricted small-self is nothing but no-self, which is identified with the true self or the universal self. The most popular koans of this category are Joshu's "mu", Hakuin's "sound of one hand", and the Sixth Patriarch's "original face of oneself".

Q: I have heard that there are many koans. Can you attain enlightenment by passing just one koan if you perceive it clearly, or should you work on all of them in sequence, as if going from grade school to university?

A: A koan is an expedient means by which to attain enlightenment. For the person who is able to attain great enlightenment by one koan, one koan is enough. In the same instant that Shakyamuni Buddha saw the morning star, he attained enlightenment. Passing through one gate, he passed through a thousand gates at the same time. We call this seeing everything at a glance. That is to say, when you see one thing clearly, you see thousands and millions of things at the same time.

To realize the structure of life in one glance, however, is very difficult; in fact, it is impossible unless you have an innate ability to do so. Even such great masters as Master Hyakujō and Master Rinzai had to go through more than one enlightenment; that is, they did not immediately see everything in one glance. (There are various degrees of enlightenment depending upon the clarity of perception or vision). Before attaining great enlightenment, both masters—ever deepening and clarifying their initial enlightenment experiences—had several enlightenments, or several glimpses into the nature of Reality.

The ten ox-herding pictures depict the various stages in attaining enlightenment. Such a division into ten steps, or stages, does not really exist. When we speak of the various stages of enlightenment, we only do so as a metaphor for the enlightenment experience, which, in essence, is inexpressible.

Buddhism is understood as the teaching of "turning delusions into enlightenment", and "turning consciousness into wisdom". The principle of *yuishiki* or "mind only", describes the eight kinds of consciousness of the human being: eye, ear, nose, tongue, and body consciousness. The sixth is mind consciousness, which perceives external phenomena; the seventh is *mana* consciousness, which is based on the idea of the "I", or ego. There is also an eighth consciousness called *alaya* consciousness, in which all sorts of experiences—good and bad, right and wrong— are stored.

These eight kinds of consciousness turn into the four wisdoms: the great, round mirror wisdom; fundamental wisdom; subtle observation wisdom; and spontaneous action wisdom. Enlightenment exists when these transformations take place.

The most stubborn and strong consciousness is the seventh consciousness. As long as you have a self-centered view of the ego, you cannot understand what Buddhism really is. The first step towards understanding is to transform the I-consciousness into fundamental wisdom, or the wisdom of prajna. This is the reason why Zen practice emphasizes work on the Dharmakaya *(hosshin)* koans which enable you to realize the prajna wisdom.

The Dharmakaya koans are very difficult to pass. When you pass your first Dharmakaya koan, or your first barrier, turning your I-consciousness into fundamental wisdom, it is said that you have had kensho. You will realize what kensho is when you actually experience it yourself.

In the state of oneness, the mountain is no longer high, the ocean no longer deep, the willow tree loses its green color, flowers lose their red color.

Since this state is an exceedingly wonderful one, once you realize it you may become attached to it. To avoid forming an attachment to this state of oneness is a real problem following one's first kensho experience.

When you work hard and do not become attached to this highly desirable state of oneness, you begin to perceive differences in the oneness. After the state of fundamental wisdom becomes deeper, once more the willow tree is green, the flowers are red. When you are still in a deluded state before kensho, you have discriminative vision based on the ego. After you attain enlightenment, you also perceive distinctions, but the distinctions are now viewed through the wisdom of subtle observation. The difference between these two perceptions of phenomena, before and after enlightenment, is like that between mud and cloud. After enlightenment, the colors become subtle colors, the sounds, subtle sounds, taste, subtle taste, and mind becomes subtle mind. This is called the wisdom of subtle observation.

When you first attain enlightenment, you perceive the equality, or oneness, of everything; in other words, first, the Dharma-body, or oneness, then the appearance, or the difference.

Everything has its own body, appearance, and function. If we do not put our understanding into practice, if we do not make our realization function in everyday life, then it is useless. This functioning, freed from conditioning, enables you to accept everything as it is and to react to everything in a natural way. This is the fourth wisdom, the wisdom of spontaneous action.

Among the koans, there is one which says: "Pull the five-storey pagoda out of the teapot". When you are able to handle this sort of koan without any hesitation, you can act freely in any situation. In your daily life, whatever you do becomes the Buddha's action, and the Buddha's conduct. The perception of oneness, or fundamental wisdom; the perception of the differences, or subtle observation wisdom; the perception of the refined functioning of the five senses, or spontaneous action wisdom, are three, and yet one. The three wisdoms together comprise the great mirror-like wisdom. There are degrees of understanding, ranging from shallow to profound, in realising these four wisdoms and in realizing their interrelationships.

It is when we attain Great Enlightenment that we can truly appreciate the life of wisdom which is like a clear, full moon illuminating the heavens.

In Zen we say that we do not depend on words or letters, for Zen transcends all verbal expression. Nevertheless, we have many verbal expressions. There are numerous records in which are found sayings, gathas, capping phrases, commentaries, and interpretations. The system of koan study originated by Master

Hakuin includes the five teachings of the Tendai School (that is, the five periods into which the Tendai Sect divides the teachings of the Buddha). Besides these five basic teachings, koan study also includes elements of Taoism, Shintoism, and poetry.

All our actions and conduct in life become the realization of the koan. There is no end to koan practice, especially in the practice of lay Zen. There is a boundless expansion of the creative process. It becomes possible for us to lead a highly aware and awakened life within the common ordinary life.

In koan practice certain koans are more appropriate to work on depending on the career of the individual, or on the structure of his daily life. Of course, the most suitable koans to work on are those which have a close connection with our daily lives. In order to deepen our understanding, we must work on the koans for a long time, trying hard to realize and actualize them in our lives.

Q: There are basically two different kinds of Zen, shikan-taza and koan Zen. What is the difference between them?

A: When Shakyamuni Buddha attained enlightenment, he exclaimed: "How miraculous! How miraculous it is! All sentient beings have the wisdom and virtue of the Tathagatha."

If you are able to accept this proclamation by Shakyamuni Buddha and realize it completely, you do not need to practice, since you are already aware of your Buddha-mind and are already able to pursue an enlightened life. Dōgen Zenji, in fact, deeply questioned why we must practice at all if we are already enlightened. He left Mount Hiei, the center of the study of Buddhism at that time, and went to visit Master Eisai at Kennin Temple in Kyōto. After Eisai's death, he studied with Myōzen who had received the Dharma from Master Eisai. Then, accompanied by Myōzen, Dōgen Zenji went to China to seek the Dharma. In China he studied under Master Nyojō, and realized that zazen is the Dharma-gate to liberation from attachment to body and mind. Having liberated his body and mind, Dōgen Zenji returned to Japan.

According to Master Dōgen, zazen is not an expedient means by which you attain enlightenment, but rather the Dharma-gate to the liberation of body and mind, and the actualization of enlightenment.

Dōgen Zenji emphasizes the importance of shikan-taza and of having faith that practice and enlightenment are one. He tells us to practice with such an attitude, even before we actually attain enlightenment.

Buddhism views enlightenment from two different perspectives: as original enlightenment, or as enlightenment through practice. Master Dōgen emphasizes shikan-taza and original enlightenment. In other words, he believes that practice and enlightenment are one. Practice is enlightenment, enlightenment is practice.

There is no doubt that by having firm faith we can best develop, as well as sustain, deep samadhi power. Time ripens and the liberation of body and mind is realized. Life, once we have liberated body and mind, becomes the manifestation and functioning of prajna. When this happens, our life is in harmony with the Dharma. In the Soto School, form itself, carrying the spirit of the Dharma, is the manifestation of the Dharma.

There are, however, very few people advocating oneness of practice and enlightenment who continue to sit until they actually attain enlightenment—even though they may have great faith. Often when people have profound faith and a good intellectual understanding of the teachings of Buddhism, they are satisfied to remain like that.

In the Soto School there are many fine scholars, as well as great masters, who have very strong samadhi power. A very limited number, however, really sit, and relatively few become creative, vital forces in their culture.

Koan Zen emphasizes the attaining and experiencing of enlightenment, the turning of delusions into enlightenment. It is all right to start with questioning and doubting. In fact, it is said that the greater the questioning or doubting, the greater the enlightenment.

The point is how to become enlightened. This is where koan study comes in. The word koan literally means a government document or a case in the Supreme Court. Since these koans are very authoritative, cases of similar nature are referred to them. Many masters have used koans to attain great enlightenment.

Koan study serves as a firm foundation for our practice and makes it easier for us to improve it. It is said that there are seventeen hundred koans. Actually, there are as many koans in life as there are individuals, and each individual's life is filled with koans. He is able to work on them wherever and whenever he wishes to. It is necessary, however, to deal with them seriously.

Koan study provides us a chance to sit more intensely. In our study of koans, we also ought to have *sanzen,* or dokusan, with a teacher. Samadhi power, or the power of concentration, is an inevitable by-product as we try to solve the koans without letting go of them at any time.

When you start studying koans, and pass a few of them, you may feel that you understand Zen. You may even become arrogant and conceited. Self-satisfaction, whether it occurs in the beginning stages of koan practice or after you have completed koan study, impedes further progress.

Both shikan-taza and koan study have advantages and disadvantages. If possible, it is better to first study koan zen in order to see clearly the fundamental problems or questions in Zen and become capable of handling them. After finishing koan study, you may deepen and refine your understanding by shikan-taza. In this way I believe that you will become a true Zen student, who has the right realization and wisdom—one who is able to freely utilize his understanding in everyday life. It is my firm belief that such a one will be able to offer a great contribution by bridging the gap between the cultures of the East and West. I really hope that many such people will appear in the future.

CHAPTER 8
"Jōshū's Dog"
Kōryū Ōsaka Roshi

The Case*

A monk once asked Jōshū, "Has a dog the Buddha-Nature?"

Jōshū answered, "Mu!"

The Commentary

For the practical study of Zen, you must pass the barriers set up by the masters of Zen. The attainment of this mysterious illumination means cutting off the workings of the ordinary mind completely. If you have not done this and passed the barrier, you are a phantom among the undergrowth and weeds. Now what is this barrier? It is simply "Mu", the Barrier of the Gate of Zen and this is why it is called "The Gateless Barrier of the Zen Sect."

Those who have passed the barrier are able not

---

*R.H. Blyth, trans., *Zen and Zen Classics, Vol. IV: Mumonkan* (Japan: The Hokuseido Press, 1966), pp. 22, 31-32.

only to have an intimate understanding of Jōshū, but also of the whole historic line of Zen Masters, to walk hand in hand with them, and to enter into the closest relation with them. You see everything with the same eye that they saw with, hear everything with the same ear. Is not this a blessed condition? Wouldn't you like to pass this barrier? Then concentrate your whole body, with its three hundred and sixty bones and joints, and eighty-four thousand hair-holes, into this Question; day and night, without ceasing, hold it before you. But do not take it as nothingness, nor as the relative "not" of "is" and "is not". It must be like a red-hot iron ball which you have gulped down and which you try to vomit, but cannot.

All the useless knowledge, all the wrong things you have learned up to the present, — throw them away! After a certain period of time, this striving will come to fruition naturally, in a state of internal and external unity. As with a dumb man who has had a dream, you will know it yourself, and for yourself only. Suddenly your whole activity is put into motion and you can astonish the heavens above and shake the earth beneath. You are just as if you had got hold of the great sword of Kan-u. You meet a Buddha? You kill him! A master of Zen? You kill him!

Though you stand on the brink of life and death, you have the Great Freedom. In the four modes of the six rebirths you are in a state of peace and truth. Once more, how are you to concentrate on this Mu? Every ounce of energy you have must be expended on it; and if you do not give up on the way, another torch of the Law will be lighted.

CUSTOMARILY speaking, in Japan, when we have the Great Sesshin, such as this, which lasts for a week, we first have a short sesshin, three or four days in length, to prepare for the Great Sesshin. When you climb mountains, you can't climb a high one from the very beginning without preparation. Rather you first climb lower mountains to acquire the techniques and other knowledge which are necessary for climbing higher peaks. The same thing can be said for the practice of zazen. It is rather difficult to work on a koan right away. Your body, breath and mind should be adjusted and controlled, and be prepared first. By so doing you can then effectively work on your koan. Zazen improves and progresses almost endlessly. From the beginning it is very difficult to do good zazen. However, your body and mind must be very well adjusted to start with.

In order to adjust your body and mind ideally, in other words, in order to be really ready to go, two or three days should be spent in either counting the breath, or following the breath, by which you can create a very harmonious, steady condition in both mind and body. For those who are sitting daily, it is advisable to practice counting the breath, and following the breath for the first few minutes of each sitting. Then, having adjusted yourself well, start working on your koan. This is always a wise way to practice zazen.

Before we get into this koan, I should like to say a word about Jōshū. He lived in China about 1200 years ago and was the 10th successor from Bodhidharma.

When he was a teenager, he studied under Master Nansen. Master Nansen asked Jōshū, "Where did you come from?", and Jōshū replied, "I am from Zuizō". Then Master Nansen asked him, "Did you go to pray to the Great Buddha in Zuizō?", and Jōshū replied, "No Sir, the Great Buddha is in front of me, lying down on the floor." The Master Nansen asked him, "What are you talking about?" And Jōshū said: "My great teacher, I am very pleased that you are in good spirits and good health."

Zen has nothing to do with past or future, but always it directly deals with the moment right now.

When he was 18 years old he had satori, but for 40 years after he attained enlightenment, he stayed with Master Nansen and served him. When Jōshū was 57 years old, Master Nansen passed away. After his teacher's death, Jōshū stayed three years in order to have memorial services for him. And when Jōshū was 60 years old, he started to visit many masters all over China until he was 80 years old.

Before he started visiting many masters, he made up his mind. He determined: "Although a 7-year old kid knows better than I do, I will ask him to teach me, and although he is a 100-year old man, if I know better, I will teach him." Then he started to visit masters.

During these twenty years, until he became 80 years old, he visited many outstanding masters in China, and became very well trained. He took up residence in a temple, named *Kannon* in Jōshū province, and there he taught until he was 120 years old.

He never used the stick or shouted. These methods were unnecessary for him; he knew exactly what to express and how to respond. He just verbally responded to the students, whoever came, and his words were like precious jewels. We call his Zen, "Zen of lips and tongue".

A wandering monk one day appeared in front of him, and seeing a dog running around the yard of the temple, asked Jōshū, "Does a dog also have Buddha-nature?" To this question, Master Jōshū replied, "Mu". That is this koan.

When Buddha Shakyamuni attained enlightenment he exclaimed: "How miraculously wonderful it is! All sentient beings have Buddha's virtues and wisdom!" "Mu" literally means negation, nothing. The Buddha's words definitely say that all sentient beings have Buddha-nature. But we hear Jōshū's answer; he says, "No". It is a big contradiction. The answer is to be found in that contradiction.

The point of this koan, and the answer to this koan, is not in whether the dog has Buddha-nature or not. It is not a matter of the dog, it is not a matter of the answer Jōshū gave, but within yourself you have to have this clear answer.

The priest Mumon worked on this koan for six years. Since he opened his eye of wisdom by it, he named his book after it, calling it the *Gateless Gate,* and compiled 48 different koans in that book.

One night he was doing zazen, and suddenly he heard a clap of thunder. And at that instant, he attained enlightenment.

Now let us appreciate Mumon's comment, "For the practical study of Zen, you must pass the barriers set up by the masters of Zen." That is to say, in order to realize, to understand what Zen is, you must go through or pass through this koan. The very subtle dynamic state of enlightenment cannot be perceived only by a psychological interpretation. If you don't go through this koan, you are like "a phantom among the undergrowth and weeds". Now what is this barrier? It is simply 'Mu', the Barrier of the gate of Zen, and this is why it is called 'The Gateless Barrier of the Zen Sect'."

Now what are the barriers set up by the masters? That is to say, what is the koan? That of Zen Buddhism is this monosyllable "mu". When you realize what this is, you will see the Buddha Shakyamuni, not only him, but also the great masters, such as Tōzan, Rinzai and Jōshū. You will see things in the same way as they. Not only will you see them face to face and hear the same things as they hear, but also you will enjoy and go on the way hand-in-hand with them. And so priest Mumon asks us, "Is not this a blessed condition? Wouldn't you like to pass this barrier?" And he continues, "Then concentrate your whole body, with its three hundred and sixty bones and joints, and eighty-four thousand hair-holes, into this Question; day and night, without ceasing, hold it before you." That means with your whole might, with your whole concentration and effort and devotion, to question this day and night. Needless to say, this mu doesn't mean "nothing". But it is not "something" either.

When you work on this koan, try to knead it like dough when you make bread. Knead that mu in your lower abdomen. And when you do it day after day, it will create strength, energy and power within you, and with that strength you work on it again. When you work on this further, it is as though a red-hot iron ball is in your throat which you can neither spit out nor swallow. And when you continue this state, that hot iron ball burns away all delusions and illusions, miscellaneous thoughts, unnecessary thinking that bother you. Then eventually you come to the point where there is no distinction between inside yourself and outside yourself, between subjective and objective. Then you totally become One in the absolute state.

That is the state of mind in which there is no dog, there is no Jōshū, there is no self; even the whole universe doesn't exist.

When you reach that point, it is like a dumb man who dreams and tries to explain what he has dreamt but can't. And when you have that experience, you really have a state of mind in which you "astonish the heavens above and shake the earth beneath", as Mumon explained.

In China, there once was a general by the name of Kan-u who was such a strong man that when he used his sword actually no one could stand before him. When you have this experience, you can freely use the sword of wisdom by which you are able to cut off delusions and illusions and desires. And also you will become a person who freely comes and goes in the six different states of existence —heaven, hell, human, fighting spirits, hungry ghosts and animals—and can save them according to necessity.

The whole essence of work on this koan can be summed up like this: you totally become mu yourself, from morning to night. Even in dreams, even in sleep you are with mu and mu becomes yourself. That is the way to work on this koan.

When you work on this all the time, you will get very used to it, and without trying to put much effort into it you will be in that state day and night. As you maintain such a state, you eventually totally become one with mu, and you become mu yourself, and mu becomes yourself, and you become the whole universe yourself. And when you continue to maintain this state, ultimately an explosion will take place.

Mumon composed a poem on it and said: "A dog and Buddha-nature, the answer is in that question." Mu itself is the Buddha-nature, and when you thoroughly make this your own, in that moment, you realize what you are. If you fall into the sphere of dualism, even just a little bit, then you lose sight of, you lose the total meaning of this koan. That is what he says in the last two lines: "If you think in terms of duality, you lose both body and mind."

Based on his own experience, Priest Mumon has explained it to us like this. However, this sort of experience is not easy to have, and I should like to add a few more words in order to make your practice more effective.

It is always helpful to adjust your breathing. When you inhale, try to push your lower abdomen forward slightly. When you exhale, as the lung volume decreases, the diaphragm goes up. That means that the lower abdomen will slightly contract too. It is rather ideal to work on mu-ji in harmony with your breathing. When you concentrate on mu, make the breath accompany it. That is to say, when you inhale your diaphragm goes down and your lower abdomen goes slightly forward. Then keep your concentration on mu and try to hold it in your lower abdomen. You breathe the air in at the same time you concentrate on mu and hold that mu always in your lower abdomen. Then, when you exhale, still keep your attention, your concentration on mu and hold it in your lower abdomen. Remember, when you exhale, the diaphragm goes up, and the lower abdomen goes in slightly. And when you inhale again, repeat the same thing, and when you exhale, do the same thing.

This practice is not only good for concentrating on a koan, but also it creates a very healthy physical condition. The front part of your lower abdomen has the movement of back and forth, back and forth, that is, *horizontal* movement. Also your diaphragm goes down when you inhale and when you exhale, the diaphragm goes up. That is *vertical* movement. This vertical movement of the diaphragm and horizontal movement of the abdominal wall stimulates inner organs in a very comfortable way so that your body starts to function better. By doing so not only can you control your physical condition better, but also your mind, your thinking becomes more clear.

When you start practising this sort of breathing, deep in your lower abdomen, the initially slight movement of the diaphragm increases. Then according to the increased motion of the diaphragm, your breathing becomes slower. Average frequency of normal breathing is 17 per minute. As practice continues, the frequency starts to decrease. When you really improve your breathing, it becomes only a few times per minute. As you breathe like this you start feeling very comfortable; not only comfortable, it even becomes a delightful feeling and the air also becomes more tasty. This delightful feeling is created not only because of the mental condition, but even your blood, your skin, your inner organs, each functions in its best way, and these inner organs feel joy and delight.

To have satori experience is not necessarily the first aim for us. But by this practice in a firm steady way, we will improve our physical and mental condition. Then our body becomes lighter and more comfortable, and the head, mind, the conscious mind, thinking, becomes clearer and joyful. This is the first stage we should improve.

So far, as I have explained, I should like you to improve the condition of your being. And approaching the end of this sesshin, I really want you to create a strong harmony within yourself.

I conclude my talk.

CHAPTER 9
Receiving the Precepts
Taizan Maezumi Roshi

JUKAI and Bodhisattva ordination and layman's ordination: do they all mean the same thing?

A: In a way, yes. Jukai literally means to receive the precepts, and also it is used for giving the precepts, too. (In that case, the Chinese ideographs are different even though the pronunciation is the same.) That is to say, from the teacher's side, jukai means to give the precepts, and from the student's side, jukai means to receive the precepts. Bodhisattva ordination we call *bosatsu kai,* meaning the Bodhisattva precepts. Perhaps Bodhisattva ordination is not the right word to say; rather, to receive the precepts of the Bodhisattva or to give the precepts of the Bodhisattva. That is what it means. Lay ordination and monk's ordination are fundamentally the same in the Soto School: to receive the sixteen Bodhisattva precepts consisting of the Three Treasures, the Three Pure Precepts, and the Ten Grave Precepts. These sixteen precepts are the Bodhisattva's precepts. Regardless of whether layman or monk or nun, all receive this. The only difference is that the layman maintains the precepts simply being a layman, and the monk as a monk. The monks and nuns devote their time fully to accomplish their Way, which is for themselves and also for others, while the layman has a job and works in secular life and tries to accomplish and maintain the precepts, which is the Buddhist way also. That is the difference.

Q: We see a lot of American monks who are involved very much in the practice but who also have secular jobs. How do you explain this in light of what you have just said?

A: Strictly speaking, monks and nuns should not marry. I myself have married, and I understand many of them marry. In fact, unmarried monks are rare; however, strictly speaking, if we marry it cannot really be called *shukke* tokudo. We use two terms: *shukke* tokudo and *zaike* tokudo. *Zaike* tokudo refers to the layman's precepts. The term literally means "to stay home or to dwell in the family in the home". *Shukke* tokudo, the monk's precepts, means to go out from home, to cut off relations to the family as such. That is why when we have monks' ordination, or tokudo, at the beginning, we shave the head, then we chant the gatha in which we say that while we are in the stream of the three worlds we cannot extinguish the attachments, we enter the state of *mui,* no-action, and this is the way to appreciate life. However, since we have family life and we marry, somehow, we have to maintain and accomplish the Way as much as possible in the position in which we are involved, so that, even though, strictly speaking, we are not to be called monks or nuns, and yet we try to maintain the precepts as much as possible—*(laughing)*—like half-layman, half-monk. Again, as far as the interpretation goes, the important thing is to detach and make oneself free, to accomplish oneself, and also to be beneficial and helpful to others. This is the idea. Just being a monk or nun, being single, does not necessarily mean that one has reached the accomplished state. Being a monk or nun, one could be much less accomplished than a layman, and being a layman, one could accomplish far more than the average monk or nun. What makes the difference is freedom from attachment. Shaving the head means to cast away the attachments, abandoning the worldly desires. (Somehow hair is the object of very strong attachment. That we observe very easily. Somehow hair is a very easy object to which to attach.) Shaving the head, the cutting off of the hair, means to detach from

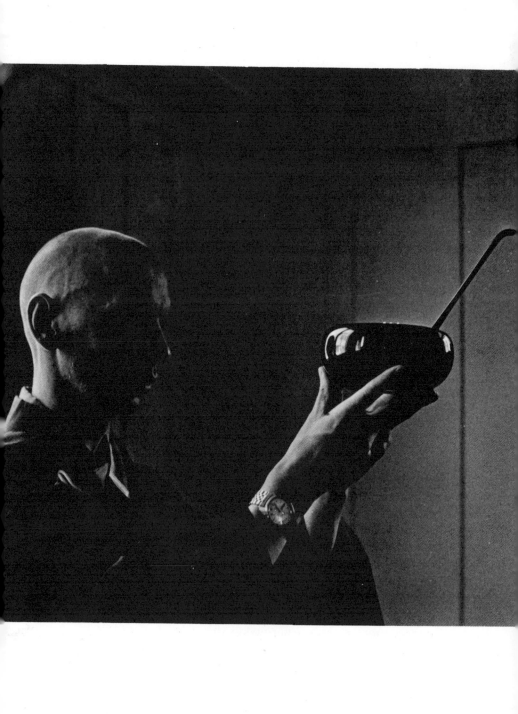

delusory things.

Q: Do you think the attachment to hair is especially strong in America?

A: I don't think so. I think it is a very common thing as a human. Then again, that means rather not only to shave the hair on the head, but rather to shave the hair of the mind, so that we try to be detached from desires. Generally speaking, we call the three poisons greed, anger, and folly. And being a layman, one is able to accomplish as much as the monks do. And even being monks with families, yet there is the possibility of accomplishing as much as the masters did.

Q: Roshi, could you explain the jukai ceremony itself. What is its structure?

A: As I mentioned previously, shaving the head symbolizes casting away worldly desires. That is the first thing you should do. The next is repentance; and again this repentance is extremely important. In any religion, I suppose, they have some form of repentance or confession. I do not know the exact implication of these terms, but here I use the word repentance. To repent in the sense we use it is not only to repent of the bad things you did yesterday or weeks ago, but rather, repentance is to make yourself one with the Three Treasures. We classify different kinds of repentance, and the genuine form of repentance is called *jissō sange*—repentance being one with reality. The Reality Repentance is what it literally means. That is to say, to identify yourself with reality. That is what it means by repentance. Of course, we have the Gatha of Repentance:

> All the evil karma ever committed by me since of old,
> On account of my beginningless greed, anger,
>   and ignorance,
> Born of my body, mouth, and thought—
> Now I repent of them all.

In the last phrase, it says, I repent of all these sins and errors. Now, that means to be one with reality. Actually that is the state of Zen. It is said that when you really repent, you make yourself one with total reality, and right there, the precepts are, in a way, able to be maintained. Then making yourself pure and unconditioned, you are ready to receive the precepts.

Q: What follows the repentance part of the jukai ceremony? *A*: After repentance, the officiant remarks that now by repentance you have made yourself pure and unconditioned, and you are ready to receive the precepts. And actually that very pure, unconditioned state, that is the state of holding the Three Treasures, fundamentally. And receiving the precepts makes that state sure, more secure, and confirms that state of purity. And first, *namu ki e butsu,* "be one with the Buddha", that is the first precept; then "be one with the Dharma" and "be one with the Sangha": these are the Three Treasures. Actually, as I described this is the very state of reality itself, so that you identify yourself with reality. That is what receiving these Three Treasures means. This is the very body of the term—precepts—actually it is reality itself. Then how it appears to be in the practice, that is next; the Three Pure Precepts. Literally it means the precept, the order. In other words, instead of simply being reality, there is also order. Then, just be that order, or identify yourself with the ordering of the universe. That is what the first Pure Precept means. Generally we say, "do not commit evil", but it is not a matter of "do not", rather it simply *cannot* be if you identify yourself with the order of the universe itself.

Q: Evil in this sense, then, actually means anything that is out of harmony with the order of reality? *A:* Out of harmony or out of order, against law, becomes sort of evil. If we explain it further, each individual has certain roles, and these roles change in accord with environment or circumstances. One person from time to time could be father, worker, friend, son, even grandfather or grandchild. According to the time and position and place, it is constantly changing. Then, in each changing circumstance, how you act and react in accord with the order or the law of the world, universe, as a human, that is what the first Pure Precept means.

Then the second one is to do good, which involves both the second one and third one, to do good for others. The second and third ones are rather positive sides of the first. To extend that goodness, not only for yourself, but for the sake of others is the very fundamental functioning of the Three Treasures, which

is reality, which is your total existence.

Then, more practically speaking, how it functions is the concern of the Ten Precepts. The Ten Precepts are a more concrete way to show how to be so. First, do not kill, again this is not simply a matter of do not kill such and such, but rather non-killing.

Q: How do you distinguish between the two? What is the difference?

A: In that genuine reality itself there is no one to kill, and no one to be killed, or nothing to be killed: such dichotomy is transcended. These Ten Precepts could be reduced to this first precept: non-killing. If one maintains this precept, actually other precepts can be well-maintained too. Dōgen Zenji comments on this. To continue or to maintain the life of the Buddha, that means not killing. Generally speaking, in order to survive we have to take some forms of life. In actual practice, we do eat vegetable, fish, even meat, from time to time. This is not necessarily killing, but rather when we interpret it, we see that we are sacrificing our life towards something else. That is how life goes. We take all sorts of life in order to maintain ourselves, and also, we offer our life towards something else. In our case we offer our life, we serve our life, towards the realization, towards the Buddha-way. Then it is not a matter of killing or of sacrifice, but rather to serve, to dedicate, to offer. And by doing so life goes smoothly. In our case, not to kill means to maintain the life of the Buddha. That is what it is.

Q: What do you mean by the phrase: "To maintain the life of the Buddha"?

A: It could mean anything—to realize your true self, to maintain the life of the Buddha, the Dharmakaya Buddha. We can say everything is the Buddha, such as, time is the life of the Buddha, do not waste time; and each time you are wasting time, you are killing the life of the Buddha. Even a scrap of paper, if you carelessly discard the value of it, then you kill the life of Buddha too. And the more your awareness increases, you become more careful, meticulous, to maintain these precepts. By doing so, things go very smoothly. It is simply because there is no friction, no conflict, with the order or the law of existence.

After you receive the sixteen precepts, the officiant remarks that the sixteen precepts have been handed down by masters, generation after generation, to the officiant; it is then given to the one who is receiving jukai. To receive jukai, to receive the precepts, means to actually confirm oneself as one with the Buddha, as the child of the Buddha, so that when the child grows up, he becomes Buddha. That is why at the very end of the tokudo ceremony, we quote the gatha from the *Bommōkyō Sutra* which says: When all sentient beings receive jukai, they enter into the sphere of the Buddha (which is the same as the state of enlightenment), and truly become the children of the Buddha. This tokudo ceremony contains terrific significance.

Q: What is the significance of the ceremony?

A: Let me use an analogy: nowadays it is fairly common for young couples to live together before marriage. So we can easily imagine such a couple living together. They may do this for quite some time; months, even years may pass. One day they realize that they have a very good relationship and are quite happy together. They may feel that they want to spend the rest of their lives together. And yet, somehow, something else remains for them to do. Once they are quite clear in their minds as to how they feel about being together, they may very well wish to formally become man and wife.

Now, this is the point: the mere act of getting married does not automatically create the relationship. But once the relationship has been established, it is quite natural to want to publicly affirm it, to make it not only a private matter, but to extend this relationship into its place in society. The formal marriage is thus very significant, since it clearly marks the formation of a family, and establishes a lineage for the children of such a couple. And further, such a public declaration of their union may serve to encourage and strengthen the couple in their life together.

Of course, if the marriage is hasty or ill-founded, then all the ceremonies in the world cannot give it life. But if the truly serious and clear-minded commitment is there, then the act of getting married is a natural expression of the couple's inner state, and arises from it quite appropriately.

To receive the precepts is, for the follower of the Buddha-way, similarly important, natural, and significant.

Q: During the ceremony, the person who is receiving the precepts is given a *rakusu* by the officiant. What is the significance of the *rakusu?*

A: Rakusu is a symbol of the Buddha's robe. Since you have become a member of the Buddha's family, you wear the clothes of the Buddha, then make yourself be aware of being a family member of this band, that is what it means; and also at the same time the Buddhist name and.the blood lineage is given.

Q: What is this blood lineage? At the jukai ceremony we see the lineage chart that the officiant presents. What exactly is that? *A:* That is handed down from Shakyamuni Buddha till, for example, myself, and when one receives the transmission of the Dharma, actually it is given to one, for example in this case, to the officiant. Thus the officiant is able to give the blood lineage to the student. But this does not mean the transmission of the Dharma to the student: rather it simply signifies the blood lineage of the officiant from whom you receive jukai.

Q: What then is the nature of the relationship, or the karmic link, between the teacher who administers the precepts and the one who receives them? Is it a very exclusive kind of relationship? Does it mean the student should not study with any other teachers?

A: Not at all so. To receive this tokudo is one thing: that simply means to become a member of the Buddhist family, and the officiant is the person who officiates at that ceremony. We call him *jugoshi,* and that means to give tokudo ceremony. After that, the student spends years of practice, finally receives the Dharma lineage, or transmission of the Dharma from someone else. That person is not necessarily the same person.

Q: I have heard about people having jukai more than once. Why would someone do this?

A: This is in a way, a very good question. Rather the renewal of the jukai. Receiving the precepts and maintaining them is not easy. Even when I reflect upon myself and my practice I feel I am almost constantly violating the precepts. That means constant repentence is necessary. Then by repenting, you make yourself new, and renew your vows. Although it sounds a little abstract, each moment you should renew your vows and precepts, and always make them anew and maintain them in a genuine way. And in the renewal of the precepts, the more you do it the better.

Again, another important matter is this: to maintain precepts is so hard that we violate them or cannot maintain them. But that does not mean we are *breaking* the precepts. There are two kinds of insufficient ways to maintain the precepts. One is to *defile* the precepts, and one is to *break* the precepts. How we distinguish them is that if you cannot put your faith in the Three Treasures any more, then you are breaking the precepts, and in that case, you are not a Buddhist any more. But on the other hand, even though you may believe, have faith in the Three Treasures, yet you may inadequately maintain the precepts (that means defiling the precepts), and in such a case, it is not really breaking them. Since they are defiled, wash them off, then they become clear, clean again. That is the functioning of repentance, and by doing so one can be again ready to maintain the precepts.

Q: Thank you very much.

CHAPTER 10
"Nansen's Cutting the Cat"
Taizan Maezumi Roshi

· At Nansen's place one day, the monks of the East and West Halls were arguing about a cat. Seeing this, Nansen held it up before them, saying, "If you can say a word, I won't cut it." The assembly made no response. Nansen cut the cat. When Nansen later told Jōshū what had happened, Jōshū took off his straw sandals and placing them on his head, went away. Nansen remarked, "If you had been here, you could have saved the cat".*

As you know, this is a very famous case. This case appears in the *Blue Cliff Record,* the *Book of Equanimity,* and the *Gateless Gate.* In the *Book of Equanimity,* from which I have translated this selection, it is one case, as in the *Gateless Gate;* in the *Blue Cliff Record,* this case is divided in two and is handled as two cases. One is "Nansen's Cutting the Cat", which is Case 63; the other is "Jōshū's Straw Sandals," Case 64.

---

*Taizan Maezumi and Dana Fraser, trans., *The Book of Equanimity* (In preparation).

Nansen and Jōshū had similar instances of awakening, and these instances are very much like that of Mumon, the compiler and author of the *Gateless Gate.* Mumon realized himself by working on Jōshū's mu-ji. It's about the dog! This case is about the cat! The real point is not whether the dog has Buddha-nature or not, or whether the cat is killed or not. What is the problem? If you say the problem is the cat, where is that cat?

I remember I talked about this case at least a couple of times previously. I think some of you remember. It reminds me that a member's mother complained about it. "The master killed the cat, how awful!" she said. In a way it is awful. On the other hand it is not awful at all. As a matter of fact, is there anything to cut off? We have to cut off the perceiving of externals-as-apart-from-everything-else, which is in fact the real cat, the real dog! That *is* the true nature. That is the cat which can't be cut in two. That's the dog which is mu! What Nansen is doing here in this case is letting the monks realize that.

In this case, maybe we'd better reflect on the precepts that we have. A number of you have received the precepts. The first of the ten grave precepts is "do not kill," or non-killing. Now "do not kill" is not really the right translation. Of course, when we look at the precepts there are different dimensions to appreciate. There is the Hinayanistic viewpoint, a purely literal perspective. You should not kill so much as an insect, even a mosquito. If you kill anything, you violate that precept. From a Mahayanistic standpoint, it's a little different. In Dōgen Zenji's *Kyojūkaimon,* "Giving and Receiving the Teaching of the Precepts," he expresses his understanding of the first precept: "Life cannot be killed." The reason it cannot be killed is very simple and obvious. Since it is one thing, it cannot be killed. "The seed of the Buddha grows. Maintain the life of the Buddha. Do not kill life." In other words, if you do not see this wholeness, this life of non-killing, of undying, you are violating this precept. That's what Nansen is dealing with.

Now east and west. In a temple, when standing in the main entrance, the right hand side is called the east wing, the east hall, and the left side is called the west hall or west wing. The monks of the east wing and west wing are arguing, it isn't necessarily about a cat as such. It may be that the cat just happened to be the direct cause of the argument. Unfortunately, all kinds of friction and fighting are common. Even here in this small community, this small center, there's friction: monks vs. laymen, men vs. women, residents vs. the larger Sangha, and those who are more involved vs. those less involved. In a society, in a group, in a family, among friends and countries, there are all kinds of friction. So here the cat as such is rather secondary.

Now that is why I have asked you where the cat is and what kind of cat it is that we are arguing about and that we have to take care of. Even in thinking about ourselves as individuals with a body and a mind, are they really in harmony? We have all kinds of different feelings, emotions, thoughts and ideas. Are they in harmony? If not, there is a cat that should be taken care of. That's the first part of the case.

Then Jōshū came back and Nansen told Jōshū what had happened. Jōshū took off his straw sandals and placing them on his head, he went away. Nansen remarked, "If you had been here, you could have saved the cat." In a way, this second part is even more important. What we should learn and appreciate and accomplish is to be like Jōshū. The monks might have had an argument similar to the case of Jōshū's dog; they might have been debating whether a cat has Buddha-nature or not; is it enlightened or deluded, real or unreal?

For Jōshū, clarifying the dichotomies of killing and not killing, arguing and not arguing, enlightenment and delusion is totally unnecessary. Nansen's talking to Jōshū about what had happened could be considered a check on Jōshū's understanding. Nansen is checking to see Jōshū's reaction. Jōshū's state of mind goes beyond any form of explanation or description. You can appreciate it for yourself. His behavior looks crazy. The important thing for us to remember is that this kind of gesture or action sometimes misleads us into thinking that Zen requires peculiar actions. But when we really get the spirit of it, it is not at all peculiar. If you really see the absoluteness, the totality, the completeness of everything, anything, including each one of us, what Jōshū is doing is not strange, not at all peculiar.

The one with very subdued, inconspicuous, subtle practice is like a dunce, like a fool. Those who manifest enlightenment in a shining, pompous way are much too green. Jōshū is not concerned with dualistic understanding, and neither should you be: good, bad, right, wrong, enlightened, deluded, east, west, killing, saving. His action was quite natural for him. Sandals being sandals, when Jōshū placed them on his head, they didn't complain. Wearing them out, they don't complain. It's better not to say too much about a case like this. It spoils it.

We have other cases similar to this, such as "Nansen's Flower." He says that people look at flowers as if in a dream. And there is the case of Master Keizan's poem, appearing in the seventh chapter of the *Denkōroku,* "The Transmission of the Light." He describes an accomplished state as a hazy moon on a spring night, shining with a subdued and subtle light. That's what Jōshū manifested. The point of the koan is to see where the cat is, what kind of cat needs to be taken care of, and also to accomplish the Way like Jōshū.

This kind of killing reminds me of another koan, that of Master Tanka Tennen, in our lineage. He was a very famous master and a bit eccentric. The occasion of his becoming a monk is interesting. His teacher was Sekitō Kisen. One day he was on his way to have an examination, like a Civil Service Exam. It was a very difficult examination. If you passed that exam, your career and status were almost guaranteed. On the way to the exam, he met Sekitō, and Sekitō asked, "Which would you like to become, an established government officer or a Buddha?" Right there he decided to become a monk and forgot that he was going to go to the examination. Right there he shaved his head and became a monk. He's the one that burned the Buddha and warmed himself up. In a way it's an awful thing to do, and yet you have to see his intention. By burning the statue of the Buddha, his intention was not to make himself warm. Rather he wanted the monks of that temple and the abbot to realize that nothing is accomplished by just paying homage to an image outside themselves. It's told that one of the monks asked, "How come? What are you doing?" "I'm trying to find the relics, the remains of the Buddha," he replied. "If it's a Buddha, it's supposed to have relics. I'm looking for them." That's really a stinging remark. It's just like the cat. What we are arguing about, what we are looking for—unless we really realize it—is just killing the cat, as well as killing our lives, and the life of the Buddha.

Engo, the compiler of the *Blue Cliff Record,* composed capping phrases for this: "The bandit is long gone; the arrow is sent."

"It is already a second-hand solution."

"Even before the cat is picked up, I'll strike him."

"If you are not like him (Nansen), you are fiddling with mud."

Our practice can be endlessly refined and accomplished. Let's practice well together.

CHAPTER 11
Dharma Dialogue: On Monk and Lay Practice
Tetsugen Glassman Sensei

GOOD EVENING. Tonight we are having *shōsan*. Basically *shōsan* is a time when we can talk together in the zendo. Dokusan is a time when the roshi and student talk privately, study together privately. Before formal dokusan became a zen practice, *shōsan* was common among people training together. They would meet at certain times and come up and ask the *shōsanshi* questions either because they wanted some information or to help improve their understanding. Some of these were testing questions, some were statements about how they felt and what they saw, and some were to provoke conversation.

Tonight I'd like to start off by giving a little historical background. In traditional monasteries the Dharma hall and zendo are separate. *Shōsan* is held in the Dharma hall. Here the zendo is used as a Dharma hall. The altar in the Dharma hall is always at the north end. In our zendo it is at the south end and we pretend it's the north. There are usually six places to the right of that altar called the east wing, and the people in charge of the administrative section of the monastery or training center sit there. The key people who deal with our Zen practice sit on the left side of the altar, which is called the west wing. So, first three people came up; those were the attendants. Then three people came up representing the east wing, the administrative side of the center and three people came representing the west side, the training side of the zendo. We sat a few minutes and now we are talking.

Many years ago in China, at a monastery at which a priest named Nansen was abbot, there were some monks quarreling and monks from the east side, from the east wing were arguing with the monks from the west side. These were senior people; the heads of the administrative end of the monastery were arguing with the heads of the training side of the monastery. And they were arguing over a cat. Both sides said, "That's my cat." And Nansen came along and saw them arguing and he held up the cat and he held up his knife and said, "Say a word of Zen and save this cat." Neither side could say anything. So he cut it in two.

This Sunday Robert Ryokaku Silvers, who is sitting here, is going to have *shukke* tokudo which is the ceremony for becoming a monk. He is also the treasurer of the Zen Center. So we could say he might sit in both wings. Of late I've heard many discussions among monks and involved lay-people on the meaning of *shukke* tokudo. What does it mean or who can do what? What's the administrative side, what's the training side? What's a monk, what's a lay person? Now I ask you: Give me a word, or the monks and lay people will remain in two. Please come up.

Q: *Shōsanshi,* you and I are both monks. What does it mean to you to be a monk?

A: I'll answer that in my concluding remarks, you answer that now.

Q: Somehow it's just who I am. I'm a monk. That's who I am.

●

Q: You have decided to wear black robes, I have decided not to wear black robes. What other differences do you see?

A: What other differences? Sometimes I see a person walking in the zendo in *shashu**, sometimes not in *shashu*. In a way, a very small point.

Q: Thank you for your answer.

•

Q: *Shōsanshi*, when I was a layman, in the morning I got up, washed my face and combed my hair. Now that I am a monk, I just wash my face when I get up. (Laughter) Is there any difference?

A: Did you cut off anything special?

Q: I didn't cut anything. I just wash my face.

A: Now's the time to dry it.

Q: Thank you for your answer.

•

Q: This morning I was over at Genpō's learning to wear robes and *kesa,* learning to be a monk. This evening I'm here as a layman. What's the difference?

A: Why is everyone asking me this question? (Laughter)

Q: You seem to be a good target.

A: The ceremony which you'll have Sunday will be very similar to the ceremony called *zaike* tokudo. Many people in this room have had the ceremony called *zaike* tokudo. They are wearing black rakusu. At that ceremony, and also at your ceremony, Roshi will chant a gatha which means that, whether you know it or not, in having the ceremony, you are the Buddha. It's not an insignificant gatha. In koan study one of the final things we study is the importance of that gatha and its meaning. In a way we could ask what the difference is between tokudo ceremony for the layman and tokudo ceremony for becoming a monk. You've had one ceremony and Sunday you'll have another. Monday, tell me the difference.

Q: Thank you for your answer.

•

---

*Shashu is the correct hand position when walking in a zendo, and is helpful in strengthening and maintaining one's concentration.

Q: *Shōsanshi,* was the man working in the parking lot today an administrator or a trainer?

A: Always a trainee.

Q: Me too.

●

Q: You asked Ryogen if anything special was cut away. If you asked me the same question, I'd have to say "nothing special", and that kind of bothers me because I don't see anything special about before and after becoming a monk. It's pretty much the same thing.

A: What bothers you?

Q: Seems like there should be something more. (Laughter)

A: Please cut that away.

Q: Then...?

A: One thing at a time. Cut what sticks out away and when something else sticks out cut it away. We have a grinder to keep it sharp. (Laughter)

Q: Then there's nothing left.

A: And that's when you start cutting with all your might.

Q: I don't quite understand.

●

Q: *Shōsanshi,* why are you asking this question? (Laughter)

A: I *have* to ask a question. Why are you asking that question?

Q: I was just curious as to why you asked that particular question. Why do you think it's important enough?

A: Oh, it's important. It's important for many reasons. Zen is an old tradition, and one of the things I love about Zen is that the form it takes depends on the culture it's in. The essence of Zen has nothing to do with the form, but it's natural that once we see, *clearly* understand what Zen is about, it manifests in our life, it *has* to. That's what it's all about. It's a natural process and when that happens, the form of the practice changes because our culture is different. Zen in India, China, Japan, and America will all be different and one of the things happening here is that a form of American Zen is developing. Always, when there are transitions from something that we're accustomed to, to something we don't know, there are problems. Long ago Shakyamuni said, "Everything is changing". People don't like that, and so they suffer. I hear lots of suffering over this very question. One of the reasons is that everything is changing, and the clear-cut definition of a monk that existed in a Japanese monastery doesn't exist here. In Japan, it's much clearer what a monk is; here it's not so clear. I hear lots of questions, so I brought it up here.

Q: OK, do you see any differences?

A: I see differences.

Q: Thank you for your answer.

A: Do you see the sameness?

•

Q: I see a difference within myself.

A: That's what we have to see. We have to see the sameness and the differences. Definitely there are differences; definitely there is the sameness. In all our practice it goes on and on like that. See the sameness, see emptiness and see form.

Q: Your question struck me as a very important question for me because I see a separation between myself and you as a monk, but I see that separation is within me, it's a separation I feel. For me the Dharmas *are* boundless and it's a matter of how we as individuals deal with understanding or strive for that understanding. I'm so new and so inexperienced and yet in the short months that I've been practicing I feel so different and so much stronger in my practice. When I imagine practicing ten or fifteen years, I get a wonderful feeling for the strength of practice and I can appreciate THAT difference between you and me.

A: That's no good, I'd rather feel like you.

Q: And I very much want to thank, um, everyone, everyone for practicing and being together.

A: Thank you. The freshness you talk about, that's wonderful and has to stay with you. Ten or fifteen years doesn't make any difference. That freshness or staleness, that makes a difference. It's interesting, some people after one day have that staleness. Some people after practicing for fifty years have that freshness. It's boundless what we can study and attain. And once we go from that freshness to staleness we cut off our heads. You've been practicing for a lifetime so please just keep going.

●

Q: On which wing of the monastery did Shakyamuni Buddha sit?

A: The north side. (pause) *What's* the north side? (pause) I'll give you a hint. *Look in the mirror.*

Q: Thank you for your answer.

●

Q: *Shōsanshi,* you said in the beginning of the evening, give a word, save the cat.

A: You heard me wrong but that's okay. Let's talk about it.

Q: OK, we'll talk about it. You talked about what sameness is and difference is. You sit here as *shōsanshi* and I come up. Today we were talking about our publication. You are a monk and I'm a layman, and it didn't matter whether you were a monk or I was a layman or vice versa; we just talked. It didn't even dawn on me that we were there. I was so involved in the discussion. That's one way to look at it. And yet you officiate services and I don't. That's another way to look at it. So I see sameness and I see differences. As far as deciding to become a monk or not (sigh) it doesn't matter to me anymore. I used to think about it, and now I just practice whatever I'm doing. When the time comes it will happen. The time came for me to move here; it happened and the whole universe was pushing it. The same thing will happen if and when I become a monk too. And if it doesn't that's OK.

A: Still you say it will happen.

Q: No, it won't happen . . .

A: Ryoshin, it's happening. (pause) What's happening?

Q: *Shōsan.*

A: Don't wait for it to happen. It's happening.

Q: Thank you for your answer.

•

Q: *Shōsanshi,* I'm rather bothered about Nansen's cat. It really seems that he could have found a better way to express himself than to have to cut that cat in half. He could have cut the sandal in half and Joshu could have walked off with the cat on his head. It seems kind of unnecessary, you know.

A: Let me ask you something. How do you cut one into two?

Q: You take something like scissors and you cut one side to the other.

A: How do you cut one?

Q: One what?

A: One.

Q: Well, one is just one, you can't cut one into anything.

A: Is that right? Thank you.

Q: Well I don't see what that has to do with what I asked you.

A: You don't?

Q: (laughs) Sort of.

A: That's the whole point.

Q: (long pause) OH!! (laughter) Okay!

•

Q: *Shōsanshi,* you said that if no one came up, monks and lay-people would remain two. Now people have come up. Are monks and lay-people two or one?

A: Were they ever two?

Q: I asked you (laughter).

A: I came up. So they're one.

Q: So they are one. Is that what you said?

A: That's what I said.

Cat, by Awashima Chingaku (1822-1888)
Harold P. Stern Collection, Washington, D.C.

Q: If they're one, how could you be sitting there while I'm sitting here?

A: 'Cause they're two.

Q: Now you're saying they're one *and* they're two?

A: Did I say that?

Q: Yet you said there are differences.

A: And I *believe* so.

Q: Then what is the difference?

A: The difference between one and two.

Q: But what is the difference?

A: The difference between one and two.

Q: But what is that difference?

A: What is that difference?

Q: I know my difference, but it may be different from your difference.

A: Well, knowing one's own difference is enough. It is very difficult to know someone else's difference.

●

Q: On the night before we celebrated Nirvana Day at Zenshuji Temple, I was in a house somewhere in Silverlake. I really felt very vividly that I was at a crossroads in my life. I looked at my life; I felt my life and the changes I had gone through. And I thought about coming back here the next morning, for morning service. It was going to be hard to get back here; I didn't have a car and I didn't know the way and I was tired and I was in a very strange place. I knew at that moment that I had it in me, not only not to come back that night, but not to come back to the zendo at all; not even to write. I knew that I could just leave; I felt like there was me, with my role and my friends at the Zen Center, and there was the present moment just totally, totally being shaped second by second. I was feeling like I could turn and leave. It was just equidistant, no guidelines. I could do from that moment on what I wanted to do. And then I felt something inside of me and in a way it was really strange. It was like something I kept losing, losing and forgetting, and it was very strange to feel, to feel like that again, and yet it was the most familiar place I know. And I felt that and I felt how, throughout my life, at certain times that had been with me and shaped my changes in ways that had nothing to do with my reasons or decisions per se, or any ability to do or not to do something. It was a feeling that somehow it was worth whatever I had to do to stay with that feeling; and at that moment I *really* knew that I wanted to be back at the Zen Center, and wanted to go to Zenshuji to celebrate Nirvana Day festivities. I knew that meant so much to me and that I would do whatever I had to do to get back (sobbing) to be with Roshi and to go to Zenshuji. Whatever it cost me. That's what it means to me to be a monk. (deep sobbing as he is hugged by the *shōsanshi*) Sensei, I love you so . . .

Jiun Sonja (1718-1804)

Epilogue: The Benefits of the Three Treasures from *Jiun Sonja Hōgoshū*

Translated by Taizan Maezumi Roshi
with John Daishin Buksbazen

If you don't receive the Three Treasures, many will fall into the *Three Akushu**. Having received them, even if your faith in them is shallow, you will receive the benefits of the human realm. When your faith in them is deep, you will receive the benefits of heaven. Having true faith in them, you will receive the benefits of sravakas and pratyeka-buddhas. Having complete, fully-realized faith in them, you will attain bodhisattvahood and Buddhahood. The distinction among these degrees of faith depends upon the shallowness or profundity of your faith in the Three Treasures.

When you have faith in the Buddha, casting away your body and mind, there is no mind aside from the Buddha, and no Buddha aside from the mind; there are no beings aside from the Buddha, and no Buddha aside from beings; there is no land apart from the Buddha, and no Buddha apart from the land. This is what is meant by having faith in the Buddha. When you really

---

*Three Akushu: (Sanskrit, *durgati*)—one of the hells, the world of hungry spirits or that of animals.

penetrate this, you may attain great enlightenment even before you arise from your seat.

When you have faith in the Dharma, casting away your body and mind, there is no Dharma aside from your body, and aside from your body, no Dharma; there are no beings aside from the Dharma and no Dharma aside from beings; there are no mountains, rivers, and the great earth aside from the Dharma, and no Dharma aside from mountains, rivers, and the great earth. This is what is meant by having faith in the Dharma. When you really penetrate this, you may attain great enlightenment even before you arise from your seat.

When you have faith in the Sangha, casting away your body and mind, there is no Sangha aside from yourself, and no self aside from the Sangha; there are no beings aside from the Sangha, and no Sangha aside from beings; there are no phenomena aside from the Sangha, and no Sangha aside from phenomena. This is what is meant by having faith in the Sangha. When you really penetrate this, you may attain great enlightenment even before you arise from your seat.

GLOSSARY

An asterisk (*) indicates a foreign word italicized in the Zen Writings Series. Those words of foreign origin without asterisks (unitalicized in the text) are considered to be in relatively common usage in American Zen practice.

ango (lit. "peaceful dwelling"): A practice period, usually three months in length, devoted to meditation, study, and communal work.

*anuttara samyak sambodhi (Skt): Supreme, Complete Awakening.

bodhi-mind (Skt: bodhi-citta; J: bodaishin): The mind of one in whom the desire for enlightenment has been awakened.

bodhisattva (Skt; J: bosatsu): An enlightened being who dedicates himself to helping others become enlightened.

bosatsukai (J) (lit. "a meeting of bodhisattvas"): Can be used to denote any group of Zen Buddhists who meet together for practice.

Buddha-nature: The intrinsic nature of all sentient beings, whether or not realized.

*buji Zen (J) (lit. "no-matter" Zen): An excessively casual attitude toward Zen discipline and training, based on the rationalization that since we are all fundamentally buddhas, we need not bother with practice, morality or realization.

dharma (Skt): Any thing or event.

Dharma (Skt): The teachings of the Buddha; Truth; Buddhist doctrine; universal Law.

Dharma hall: A room or building in a monastery in which the abbot gives his talks on the Dharma; also combined in most places with the Buddha hall, in which services are held.

Dharma name: The name given to someone when he or she receives precepts (jukai), thus formally becoming a Buddhist.

Dharma successor: A person designated by a Zen master to carry on his teaching lineage and authorized to hold dokusan, verify enlightenment experiences, and in turn name Dharma successors.

Dharmakaya (Skt; J: hosshin): One of the three aspects (trikaya) of the Buddha, it is the phenomenal world, in which all things are One.

*dhyana (Skt): Meditation.

Dōgen Kigen Zenji (1200-1253): After training for nine years under the Rinzai teacher Myozen, Dōgen Zenji made the difficult journey to China, where he studied with and became Dharma successor to Master Tendō Nyojo, in the Soto Zen lineage. Considered the founder of the Japanese Soto School, Dōgen Zenji established Eiheiji, the principal Soto training monastery, and is best known for his collection of Dharma essays, Shōbōgenzō (q.v.).

*dōjō (J): A training center.

dokusan (J): A one-to-one encounter between Zen student and Zen master in which the student's understanding is probed and stimulated and in which the student may consult the teacher on any matters arising directly out of practice.

enlightenment: Realization of one's true nature.

Five Desires: Money or wealth (zai), material things, including sex (shiki), food (jiki), fame (myo), and sleep (sui).

Four Great Vows: "Sentient beings are numberless; I vow to save them. Desires are inexhaustible; I vow to put an end to them. The Dharmas are boundless; I vow to master them. The Buddha-way is unsurpassable; I vow to attain it." Zen students chant these vows daily as an expression of their aspirations.

Fukanzazengi (J) (lit. "Universal Promotion of the Principles of Zazen"): A brief work on how and why to sit zazen, by Dōgen Zenji.

*gakki (J): Memorial service.

Hakuin Ekaku Zenji (1686-1769): The patriarch of Japanese Rinzai Zen, through whom all present-day Rinzai masters trace their lineage. He systematized koan study as we know it today.

*hara (J): The area of the lower abdomen which is the physical center of gravity of the human body, and which becomes a center of awareness in zazen.

*jakugo (J) (lit. "capping phrase"): A pithy expression which concisely summarizes or comments upon part or all of a koan. Zen students who work with koans are traditionally required to find jakugo as part of their koan practice, as further evidence of their understanding.

*jōriki (J) (lit. "samadhi power"): The vital, stabilizing energy arising from strong zazen practice.

jukai (J): Ceremony of receiving the precepts. A person receiving the precepts formally becomes a Buddhist and is given a Dharma name.

*kalpa (Skt:) An eon; an extremely long period of time.

Kannon (J; variants: Kanzeon; Kanjizai) (Skt: Avalokitesvara): One of the three principal bodhisattvas in the Zen Buddhist tradition, Kannon is the personification of Great Compassion, and is usually represented in the female form.

karma (Skt): The principle of causality, which holds that for every effect there is a cause, and, in the human sphere, maintains that by our actions we determine the quality of our lives, and influence the lives of others.

Keizan Jōkin Zenji (1268-1325): Fourth patriarch and co-founder, with his predecessor Dōgen Zenji, of the Soto School in Japan, Keizan Zenji was largely responsible for the spread of Japanese Soto Zen, and was particularly noted for his meticulous instructions and procedures governing virtually every aspect of monastic life.

kensho (J) (lit. "seeing into one's own nature"): An experience of enlightenment; also known as satori.

kinhin (J): Walking zazen, usually done for five to ten minutes between periods of sitting zazen.

koan (J): A brief anecdote recording an exchange between master and student, or a master's enlightenment experience. Koans are used in Zen to bring a student to realization, and to help clarify his enlightenment.

kyosaku (J) (lit. "waking stick"): A long stick, generally flattened at one end, the kyosaku is carried in the meditation hall by one or more monitors, who periodically whack sitters on the shoulders to encourage them or to help them stay awake.

Manjusri (Skt; J: Monju): The Bodhisattva of Wisdom, often depicted riding a lion, holding the sword of wisdom which cuts through delusion. Especially appreciated in the Zen sect, Manjusri Bodhisattva is the principal figure on the zendo altar. *Cf.* Kannon, Samantabhadra.

mu-ji (J): The character "mu", a negative particle used to point directly at reality and which has no discursive content. The use of the word in this sense originated with Master Jōshū Jushin (Ch: Chao-chou, 778-897) who, when asked by a monk, "Does a dog have Buddha-nature?" directly answered, "Mu!" The incident is used as the first koan in *The Gateless Gate (Mumonkan)*.

nirvana (Skt; J: nehan): In Zen practice, a non-dualistic state, beyond life and death.

*oryoki (J) (lit. "that which holds just enough"): Broadly speaking, the nested set of bowls given every monk and nun at ordination, from which meals are eaten. Strictly speaking, the term refers exclusively to the largest of these bowls. In early Buddhist tradition, this bowl was used to collect offerings when the monk or nun would go begging in the street. Nowadays, oryoki are also used by laypersons.

Patriarchs: Strictly speaking, the first thirty-four Dharma successors from Shakyamuni Buddha through the Sixth Chinese Patriarch, Daikan Eno (Ch: Hui-neng, 638-713). More generally, an honorific term used to describe any Zen master of outstanding attainment.

prajna (Skt; J: hannya): The wisdom of enlightenment.

precepts: (Skt: sila; J: kai): Teachings regarding personal conduct, which can be appreciated on a fairly literal level as ethical guidelines, and more broadly as various aspects or qualities of reality.

rakusu (J): Made of five strips of cloth and thus the smallest of the Buddhist robes *(kesa)*, the rakusu is the only kesa worn by both monks and laypersons, and is suspended from the neck by a cloth halter.

Rinzai School: The Zen lineage founded by Master Rinzai Gigen (Ch: Lin-ch'i, d. 866).

roshi (J) (lit. "venerable teacher"): A Zen master.

samadhi (Skt; J: zammai): A state of mind characterized by one-pointedness of attention; in Zen, a non-dualistic state of awareness.

Samantabhadra Bodhisattva (Skt; J: Fugen Bosatsu): One of the three principal bodhisattvas in the Zen Buddhist tradition, Samantabhadra is associated with practice and active love. *Cf.* Kannon, Manjusri.

*samu (J): Working zazen, often physical labor, in-or out-of-doors.

Sangha (Skt): Originally, the body of Buddhist monks and nuns, the term "Sangha" later came to include laypersons as well; in Zen, the harmonious interrelationship of all beings, phenomena, and events.

*sanzen (J) (lit. "penetration in Zen"): In the Rinzai tradition, sanzen is synonymous with dokusan. For Dōgen Zenji, founder of the Soto School in Japan, however, *sanzen* more broadly signifies the proper practice of zazen.

sesshin (J) (lit. "to collect or regulate the mind"): A number of days set aside for a Zen meditation retreat.

Shakyamuni (Skt) (lit. "the silent sage of the Shakya clan"): The title accorded Siddartha Gautama upon his becoming the Buddha (i.e., upon his enlightenment).

shikan-taza (J) (lit. "just sitting"): Zazen itself, without supportive devices such as breath-counting or koan study. Characterized by intense, non-discursive awareness, shikan-taza is "zazen doing zazen for the sake of zazen".

Shōbōgenzō (J) (lit. *"A Treasury of the Eye of the True Dharma"):* Masterwork of Dōgen Zenji, founder of the Japanese Soto School of Zen, it comprises some ninety-five articles dealing with a wide variety of Buddhist topics, and is generally considered to be one of the most subtle and profound works in Buddhist literature.

*shōsan (J): A formal meeting in Zen monasteries and centers in which a teacher or senior student gives a short talk and then engages in question/ answer dialogue with any who wish to challenge his understanding, ask a question, or make a comment. A kind of public dokusan.

*skandhas (Skt) (lit. "heaps, aggregates"): In Buddhist psychology, the five modes of being which, taken collectively, give rise to the illusion of self. They are: form, feeling, thought, discrimination, and perception.

Soto School: The Zen lineage founded by Masters Tōzan Ryokai (Ch: Tung-shan, 807-869), and Sōsan Honjaku (Ch: Ts'ao-shan, 840-901). The Japanese branch of this school was founded by Masters Eihei Dōgen (1200-1254) and Keizan Jōkin (1268-1325).

*sunyata (Skt): Emptiness; the ground of being.

sutras (Skt): Buddhist scriptures; the dialogues and sermons of the Buddha and certain other major Buddhist figures.

*tantō (J): Assistant to the godo; the person in charge of the operations of a zendo.

Tathāgatha (Skt; J: Nyorai): The name the Buddha used in referring to himself, it literally means "thus-come", indicating the enlightened state.

teisho (J): A formal commentary by a Zen master on a koan or other Zen text. In its strictest sense, teisho should be non-dualistic and is thus distinguished from Dharma talks, which are ordinary lectures on Buddhist topics.

"The Ten Oxherding Pictures": Of ancient origin, they represent a step-by-step guide to the bodhisattva path, beginning with the stage of searching for the ox, in which the desire to practice is awakened, and ending with the return to the marketplace, in which both enlightenment and unenlightenment are transcended, and the bodhisattva remains, freely functioning in the world of delusion. Actually, one passes through this entire cycle in each moment of practice.

Ten Spheres: The realms of buddhas, bodhisattvas, pratyeka-buddhas, sravaka-buddhas, heavenly beings, human beings, fighting spirits, animals, hungry ghosts and hell-dwellers.

*tenzō (J): Person in charge of the kitchen in a monastery or Zen center. Traditionally, the position of tenzō is considered to be one of the most challenging assignments.

tokudo (J): Ceremony of receiving the precepts. There are two kinds of tokudo: *zaike* tokudo, in which one formally becomes a lay Buddhist; and *shukke* tokudo, in which one becomes a monk or nun.

*vinaya (Skt) (lit. "discipline"): The Buddhist school which most strongly emphasizes monastic discipline as the basis of its practice; generally, the code of conduct upon which this discipline is based.

zazen (J): The practice of Zen meditation.

zendo (J): A place set aside for the practice of Zen.

Zenji (J) (lit. "Zen master"): An honorific term used to refer to a master of high rank or attainment.

INDEX

ABOUT THE CONTRIBUTORS

Kōryū Ōsaka Roshi: A lay Zen master in the Rinzai tradition, Kōryū Roshi is successor to Hannyakutsu Jōkō Roshi. His special contribution to Zen has been in his emphasis on the practice of lay persons. Kōryū Roshi is presently head of the Musashino Hannya Dōjō, and president of Shakamunikai, an independent organization of Zen Buddhists in Japan.

Taizan Maezumi Roshi: A Soto Zen priest, Maezumi Roshi is successor to masters representing three major lines of Zen teaching: Hakujun Kuroda Roshi, Hakuun Yasutani Roshi, and Kōryū Ōsaka Roshi. He is Director and resident Zen master of the Zen Center of Los Angeles, and Co-Editor of the Zen Writings series.

Tetsugen Glassman Sensei: A student of Maezumi Roshi's since 1968, Gen Sensei is Senior Training Monk and Assistant Director of Zen Center of Los Angeles, and Co-Editor of the Zen Writings series.

John Daishin Buksbazen: A student of Maezumi Roshi's since 1969, Daishin serves as Pastoral Counselor and Vice President of Zen Center of Los Angeles, and is Publishing Editor of the Zen Writings series.

Hakuun Yasutani Roshi: Ordained at the age of eleven, Yasutani Roshi studied as a young monk with several well-known masters. In 1925, after sixteen years as a schoolteacher in Tokyo, he became the disciple of Daiun Sōgaku Harada Roshi, from whom he received *inka* in 1943. Various zazen groups were soon established under his guidance, and in 1954 his Sambōkyōdan was legally recognized as an independent religious organization. Between 1962 and 1969, Yasutani Roshi made frequent visits to the United States, and in 1970, less than three years before his death at the age of 88, he named Hakuyu Taizan Maezumi, head priest at Zen Center of Los Angeles, as a Dharma successor. Like his teacher Harada Roshi, Hakuun Yasutani Roshi borrowed freely from Soto and Rinzai traditions, recommending both koan study and shikan-taza to his students.

Kōhun Yamada Roshi: President of the Board of Directors of Kembikyo Hospital in Japan, Yamada Roshi is the senior Dharma-successor of Hakuun Yasutani Roshi, from whom he received *inka* in September, 1960. Now head of the Sambokyodan in Kamakura, the independent religious organization founded by Yasutani Roshi in 1954, Yamada Roshi's zendo is especially popular with Christian clergy and students from all over the world.

Chōtan Aitken Roshi: Aitken Roshi was interned by the Japanese during World War II in the same camp as R. H. Blyth and their friendship stimulated Aitken Roshi's interest in Zen. After the war he studied with Nyogen Senzaki Sensei in California, and with Soen Nakagawa Roshi, Hakuun Yasutani Roshi, and Kōhun Yamada Roshi in Japan and Hawaii. In December 1974, Aitken Roshi received *inka* from Yamada Roshi, becoming the first Westerner to receive Dharma transmission in the Harada/Yasutani line of succession. Aitken Roshi heads the Diamond Sangha in Hawaii, which includes the Koko-an Zen group in Honolulu and the Maui Zendo.

The Paulownia leaves-and-flowers design is traditional in Japan, where in slightly different form, it serves as the crest of Sōjiji Monastery, one of two headquarters temples of the Soto School of Zen Buddhism. In the form shown here, it is the crest of Kōshinji Temple in Ōtawara, whose Abbot, the Venerable Hakujun Kuroda Roshi, was Maezumi Roshi's principal Soto teacher. In the United States, it represents Zen Center of Los Angeles, publishers of the Zen Writings series.